"The way we imagine our lives is the way we are going to go on living our lives. For the manner in which we tell ourselves about what is going on is the genre through which events become experiences."

James Hillman

FRIENDSHIP

Photographs by JED DEVINE   *Letters by* JIM DINSMORE

TILBURY HOUSE, PUBLISHERS / GARDINER, MAINE

PL. 1   DOORMAT / FRIENDSHIP LONG ISLAND

FOREWORD

This is about friendship, and Friendship, Maine.

It is a book in two parts, by two friends, Jim Dinsmore and me, Mr. Clutter and Mr. Clean, as he once called us, astrological opposites, Pisces and Virgo.

I met Jim in 1968 at the Loomis School in Connecticut, where I had just taken a job being the art department. Jim had been there a few years teaching courses in English, math, and the Old Testament.

We were friends from the moment we spoke. I remember mentioning the similarity between Josef Albers's ideas about color interaction and Norman Brown's saying "meaning is not in things, but in between." Jim smiled, and we were off and running on a conversation that continued over twenty years. I enjoyed his passion for amplifying events through association and word play, and his instinct for hearing the echoes around things. For Jim nothing was finished—it was always emerging, an ongoing revelation.

We were both young, married, and trying to figure out what we wanted to make and where to make it. We worked together on some rough, fleeting, 16 mm films. Sunday afternoons we played one-on-one basketball in the empty gym, and in early June, after the students had gone home to sailboats and summer jobs, we played tennis. Our intensity towered over our ability, and our competitive antics volleyed us back and forth between anger and hilarity.

At about this time, Jim's wife, Joan, inherited a share in a cottage on Davis Point in Friendship. One of my early visits to Friendship, and my first visit to Friendship Long Island, was as Jim and Joan's guest at a meal at Bob and Nat Pratt's. Natalie Pratt is Joan's aunt. It was several years later when my great uncle, Mike Kalette, asked me which island in Maine I went to. I asked him if he had ever been to Maine. "Only once, in the twenties. To an artist's house on an island," he said. I asked him if he had any idea how many islands there were in Maine. He persisted. I said, "Friendship Long Island." "That's the one," he said, "Arthur Crisp's house on Long Island." Arthur Crisp sold his house to the Pratt's. I have never believed in coincidence.

Jim and I started making frequent trips back and forth

from Loomis, sometimes leaving on Friday afternoon and returning Monday morning in the dark, just in time for classes. Jim knew immediately that he wanted to live on an island, and he was fortunate to find and purchase two parcels on Friendship Long Island from Delbert Cushman, an older fisherman, who was over the years to take on mythic proportions for Jim. Friendship Long Island is roughly two miles long and a half-mile wide. It is the first island out from the mainland, forming Friendship Harbor (PL. 3). On one of Jim's two parcels was a dilapidated camp that he called "George's"(PL. 2) in honor of its last occupant, George Cushman. The camp and the land became the focus of Jim's life.

I recall one weekend when Joan made the excursion to Friendship with us. We spent the night in the cottage on the mainland. In the morning, after Joan prepared a New England boiled dinner and set it to simmer all day, we headed out to the island in a small wooden skiff Jim had been given, judging from the looks of it, by a relative who was not crazy about him. We worked all day on George's. By late afternoon, the wind had blown up and whitecaps were pounding into the cove. We decided to wait a while — and a while more. We spent the night. With the wind at gale force, the short woodstove chimney seemed confused about which direction the smoke was supposed to go, allowing it to billow in with each gust. The heat from the stove had no such confusion; it left immediately through gaps between the unshingled wall boards. None of us slept, but at some point we did stand up, and slowly registered that the faint smell of bacon was us. We trudged across the island to the lobster pound and left a message for Boy Thompson, hoping he would be coming out in the Seasmoke, a small tugboat, to check on things. Eventually Boy did appear, and we ferried ourselves out to meet him in the still wicked water. Not until we opened the door of the cottage did any of us remember the New England boiled dinner cooking on the stove. Cautiously, Joan lifted the lid, and there, at the bottom of the pot, was the world's smallest corned beef — a backpacker's delight, a banquet the size of a briquette. As Jim would say, "Good, though."

The direction of Jim's life was soon apparent in the incessant moving and re-placing of flowers, trees, windows, outhouses, chimneys, and finally small buildings. Nothing was safe. Jim had a

vision of what the island and his life there could be, and his zeal and devotion regarding the smallest details and the most onerous tasks were limitless.

In 1970 I left Loomis to go to graduate school in graphic design and photography, neither of which I had ever done before. Four years later, Jim and Joan moved to Friendship with their two small children, Sarah and Stephen.

Friendship is at the tip of a finger of land that starts at Route 1 in Waldoboro and several miles later dips into Muscongus Bay. During the summer when the fishing is good, most of the men, a lot of the boys, some of the women, a few of the girls, and an occasional dog are on boats, grinding their way out into the pre-dawn dark, getting ready to haul their farthest traps at first light. Lobstering and the sea give all meaning and measure to the town and its people.

The exodus to Friendship was a risk for Jim and his family. There was no job waiting, no winterized house, no close friends. Jim had felt confined at Loomis, and the move was made as part of a conscious commitment to writing a novel. Their new home was the slightly improved George's. It had two small rooms, a rear wall of plastic sheeting, a tarpaper roof, and a small, inefficient woodstove. It did not have electricity or plumbing. It sits at the head of a cove that empties out perhaps 250 yards at low tide. This meant that at low water they had to walk through woods along the shore and down over boulders, rockweed, and the ooze of clam-flat mud to reach their dory. Maine school days start early by the standards of people "from away," and in the winter the children's boat ride to school on the mainland often began in the dark. Sarah and Stephen rarely missed a day of school. At that time the island had only two year-round residents: Ivan and Josephine Morse, whose place was just around the cove from George's. A year later, Rossie Simmons began wintering in a small camp alongside the Gut, a narrow channel between Friendship Long Island and Little Morse Island. In summer the population now swells to near seventy-five, a mix of summer people and local families.

A few years later, Jim sold two acres of dense spruce woods at the head of Deep Cove to me and my wife, Emmy. Deep Cove is just beyond the Gut and takes its name from its length, not its water, which disappears completely in extreme tides. We cleared the site during my March vacation breaks from teaching. Jim would drop trees hour after hour while Joan, Emmy, and I would struggle to keep up, stacking logs and dragging brush. With its combination of fire and ice, this was the kind of ritual work, determined by seasons, moons, or tides, that Jim loved.

Emmy and I lived with our children, Jesse and Siobhan, in a cluster of tents in the emerging clearing (Pl. 12) for twelve summers. It seemed paradise to us, coming as we did each June or July from the swelter of New Haven and later, New York. The first two years we hauled our water from a spring on Morse Island. We spent much of one summer scavenging crates and lumber from the islands for materials to build a cookshed that could house an old propane refrigerator and a campstove. The following year, we built a composting outhouse based on plans we got from a business in California called the "Shit Hotline." Our version had three windows, including a picture window in the front with a view into spruce woods. It became an island curiosity for a while, with relative strangers coming by asking to sit in it. These small projects were major undertakings for me: I grew up in a house in which everyone was uncertain about whether we had a hammer, but knew, if we did, that it was probably under the bag of baseballs in the back-hall closet. A power tool was as distant as a Democrat. (Things have changed. It turns out there was a Democrat in the closet, too, and I have come out. Now, of course, my father would love to find the hammer.)

Like most island summer people, I suffer the anxiety of making an ass of myself around wharves, which is silly — why should wharves be any different than any other place? I have had my initiatory debacles, none worse than when I started up our new outboard, turned to make sure the stern was clear, put it in gear, gave it the gas, and propelled the bow up and halfway across the town float— all the while gazing confidently backwards.

Through all of this, Jim acted as guide, navigator, mechanic, carpenter, host, weatherman, gardener, and companion. We were his students in a way, and I was slow to master much of the material.

After that first winter at George's, Jim took a job as a live-in caretaker at a lobster pound on Little Morse Island. His duties were to have been minimal, consisting primarily of his and Joan's visible presence. The text for Friendship is a series of excerpts from letters Jim wrote to me beginning that first winter on Little Morse with an account of a night fire in the generator house. The letters are filled with holidays, weather, people, humor, boats, construction, hunting, difficulty, and death. There is a lot of dying. As fate would have it, many of Jim and Joan's neighbors — Ivan, Rossie, Raymond Cushman, Merritt Post, Delbert Cushman, and Boy Thompson, all died in a matter of years, collapsing one after the other like the pilings of an old wharf. I looked forward to Jim's letters but came to fear the prospect of yet another loss, and I began to feel that the passing of these men signaled the end of a way of life.

Over time, Jim became increasingly consumed with the house he was building around the original George's, which he had taken apart board by board and meticulously reassembled. This work brought him into regular contact with the townspeople whom he came to admire deeply and began to recreate for his novel. But the novel was to remain largely imaginal, existing in the form of stacks of boxed notes. The effort on the house crowded out his resolve to push the book along. It became obvious that Jim was producing more chimneys than chapters. This awareness haunted him, and his various herculean projects were never able to dispel its ghost. His writing took the form of extended letters to friends. Jim's last letter to me was in 1988, not long before he was operated on for a brain tumor. The doctors were optimistic and gave him ten years. He died ten weeks later on my birthday.

Jim and I never worked on this book together. In fact, he probably saw no more than a handful of the sixty-four pictures, and several that he refers to in his writing are not included here. I had been thinking about a book for years, and Jim and I had agreed that he would write something specifically to accompany the images. That was not to be. Even after I decided to use parts of his letters for the text, I never made images to illustrate what he had written about.

The letters are incomplete, intermittent, and full of gaps. People and events bob up to the surface and then disappear beneath it. Reading the letters is akin to walking the shoreline, picking up what interests us and building with an accumulation of fragments a sense of the cycles of loss and return. And like treasures we lift from a beach's welter, the letters evoke, from what is present, feelings for what is not.

As time went on, Jim's letters got longer and denser. In one of them he compares Delbert Cushman and James Joyce in their genius for dealing with complexity. He points to Delbert's fisherman's gift for undoing "a fathom's looped up tangle" and to Joyce's "looping lines and tangle" as "complex, jewel-like, underwater refractions." I remember thinking when I read this that Jim was also describing himself. I love his description of Joan falling off of George's roof "like a frogman over the gunwale into water," and of Harold Benner sitting in his shop, Ahab-like, "with the mutilated patience of a whaleman," and of a frigid January night when it seemed possible "that nothing will ever move again, that everything will stay forever put, or else shatter at the least touch," and of the view from the dory, with Sarah in her clam costume, of "the distant houses above the harbor, where we could see Halloween's extra lighted doorways, promising, purposeful, like the fleshy, hot interiors of jack-o-lanterns." These are among the pleasures that Jim's writing brought tidelike to my door once or twice a winter, and that, for reasons I did not understand at the time, I saved. Jim struggled, like most of us, with what Mary Oliver, in her poem "Spring," says is the only question: "how to love this world." I believe he found a partial answer in his writing.

There is a lot in the letters that is not in the photographs and vice versa. Most of Jim's letters were written in the winter and most of my pictures were made in the summer. Writing and photography are as polar as opposite seasons and signs, but, as complements, each can provide something that the other can not. This is the dynamic of the book, and where connections exist they are achieved more by resonance than reason. Like fishermen, we worked the same water but set our own traps. This is our haul.

I decided, after originally structuring the book with the text and images interwoven, that they were better off, like friends, side by side. The letters are in chronological order, and an ellipsis indicates where sections have been omitted. I use an 8"x10" camera and my prints are palladium contacts. The photographs were made over many years as the wooden traps in some of the pictures clearly show. I try to make images that hold something of the light and the dark I have both seen and felt. Developing an extended sequence from images that were made as individuals was a labor full of surprises that concluded, as you might expect, with the pictures finding their own places. In keeping with Norman Brown's "there is no literal truth," there is no attempt to make an objective documentation of the town or of our lives here. It is closer to a musing and a meditation; an attempt to honor the sensual and spiritual reality of this place. I agree with Jorge Luis Borges: "Everyday places become, little by little, holy."

From Loomis I went south to New Haven and New York and Jim went north to the island. But it didn't matter. If I was mushrooming in the island woods, trolling for mackerel between Otter and Cranberry, loading wood at Fred Storer's lumberyard, or just sitting in camp with a "honk" of whiskey, Jim would often appear. We seemed to end up together even when we were going in different directions. His words, my images: I think they are like that.

JED DEVINE

. . . and in his mind, the cars still slipping by on U.S. 1 in strung-out regiments gone somewhere, to look at the leaves, the brilliant fallen — whole families packed up, calling it "vacation," holy days, filled with fantasies and framed visions, and a camera to make it all real with and take home, untouchable, suspended in time and space like gathered trophies. And overhead where he stood as always there, in Maine, the big jets heard slipping by, winged horses, way up, coursing up the coast like Pegasus, and out, gone to Europe and back, but heard from where he stood only as fading hoarse whispers among the stars, a sound of fled dreams returning, and even the sense, slipping by, below and out to sea, of the armies of summer mackerel in the bay — neither seen nor heard at all, but known by now, in October, to have slipped back out to sea according to some felt need, a rhythm of the universe. And so what then, amidst all that, was he — standing fixed among all that he had left or come to — cars, airplanes, great crowds in motion — even the fish — what was he doing there? — just there, and with a sense of things slipping by, and alone, immobile, fixed among the motions of his mind . . .

From Jim's unfinished novel

Pl. 2   Jim at "George's" / Friendship Long Island

L E T T E R S

Wednesday night I watched the Red Sox lose the Series, slept alone at the pound. Woke up for some reason around 2 A.M. noticed an orange glow out the big window, went out and found the generator house filled with fire. Couldn't believe it. Strange calm black night all alone, raging fire out of nowhere, sleep. Went back inside, wanting to turn it off, like bright lights left on. No phone (no power), no boats going by. Got clothes on, shaking all over. Rossie's light not on. Outside again, through the shop door, and the heat there now as from suddenly behind a shield. Ran screaming along the fence — Rossie — help — help help — help — Rossie — fire — Rossie! Screaming all the way over to Rossie's in the dory. Banging on the door, him swearing, muttering, blubbering things back. Looked out his window: can't do nawthin', watch it go, that's all. Flames way up — over the roof, the whole place lit up. He thought the whole house was on fire. Rossie, take me to the mainland. He didn't want to. Why can't you go? My dory's too slow. Take my boat. I can't run it. Sure you can. I'm not going. Wait a minute. Goddammit. Running out on the wharf to his offhaul. Waiting for him. Fire wild from there even, the whole pound will go. Gasoline cans, barrels, engines exploding across there, popping off like rifles. Shotguns, night hunters. Wham — wham! No one there. Could see the flames spreading out along the wharf, fast, like water spreading out. Rossie got his boat. Where's your dory? Tie up your dory. I watched the fire from the bow of his boat as he went out along the gut (PL. 9). A miracle if the house didn't go with it. Twenty feet away. Could see things falling, part of the roof maybe. Then the diesel tank: had been waiting for it, hanging still on the wall, black patch in all

Rossie Simmons (PL. 8) lived in a small camp along the Gut. The sparkle in his eyes was a clear indication that he was younger than his eighty-odd years. There was a quiet, resigned strength about Rossie that I am not sure I have come across before or since. He carved boats and decoys and watched traffic in the Gut with the attention and interest most Americans lavish only on soap operas and TV talk shows. He had a zen grace for living simply and happily.

that flame, as if silhouetted in the light, big 200 gallon tank. Sounded like a cannon, or a bomb, and it must have spread fuel all over the water in that part of both pounds, because when Rossie came back maybe fifteen minutes later he said the whole surface of the water in the pound from there down was on fire. It drifted against the fence that separates the pounds. I came back on Albert Simmons's boat with 15 or 18 firemen, portable equipment, lights, radios, and later a firemen's wife said it was 22 minutes between the phone call and landing at the pound. Somebody even brought a bag of apples. Really impressive. The house would have gone up if they hadn't come, and if there had been a stiff wind, the island itself would have burnt, the trees across the pound — Post's house . . . was like a blowtorch firing straight up into the air. Burning oil, fuel. A creosote barrel blew itself all over the water. By 4:30 everybody had left, big high white moon overhead, black silent sky, no boats yet, no wind. I took the rowing dory back to the other end of the pound. The firemen had used it. Rowing, the tide going, and in the darkness I couldn't even see the change, except no generator house, couldn't see the rubble, couldn't smell smoke, couldn't smell the oil I was rowing in. Back to bed, alone. Didn't sleep. An hour later, someone whistling softly by my window. Still black, moonlight night. Johnny, Boy, Henry, Ikey. Johnny said: Gawdammit Jim! The next time you decide to have a weenie roast you call me.

NOVEMBER 21, 1976

The love and friendship of your letter moved us a very

Merritt Post owned, operated, and to a large extent built the lobster pound on Little Morse Island, which he later sold to Coastal Fisheries. An eccentric, energetic adventurer from outside New York, Merritt was entertaining, charming, and thorny. He flew his own seaplane, with his dog, Drift, as copilot. With the sound of their approach, those of us on that side of the island would run to hilltops or clearings along the shore to watch their unpredictable landings in the Gut.

great deal. It is too easy for me at least to forget that, being "alone" here, we are separated so much of the time from people like you we love — and need. I don't forget that we are separated from people; but I seem to "forget," emotionally, that there are needs and warmths that I am doing not very much about. I have seemed to treat my need to write in somewhat the same way, too. Not doing it, knowing that it's there — and not doing it for reasons I can't even explain any more except that I am afraid of it now, it has been so long — not doing it. I seem to prefer the long and empty depression. Your kindness in sending even just your love — and all the memories and associations around you — came as a kind of glimpsed joy.

Whatever little hell I am living in my interiors here at present is very personal, I think — I am responsible in a way I have never before had to reckon with.

FEBRUARY 23, 1977

A neat idea, that you are thinking about coming here next month. The days are already getting noticeably longer, fast, and even occasionally, like today, early spring glorious weather. Can feel the sun now. But still enough winter to be winter, other times. Changes. March can blow a lot, but boat can handle it. Scallops will still be in season, so if we get a good day (calm) with tide right, that might be fun. This spring I'm going to get a trawl and go out for "ground fish" — hake, haddock, cod, pollock, flounder, etc. — maybe even halibut. Should be fun and not a hell of a lot of work. Nice way to have a day out. Out one day to set the trawl (25-50 hooks), then back a day or two later to haul it — bait it and reset. Out between Allen's Head and Monhegan. Ivan has fixed up, rebuilt, my old hauler, and I'm going to mount a mast and boom on the boat, so we'll be able to drag for scallops too. Which brings to mind: did I tell you that she is being documented by the U.S. Coast Guard as the "G/S ALDA E," sailing out of Rockland, hailing from Friendship? A guy from C. Guard in Boston came up and measured her all up and down, drew diagrams, then wrote me a couple of weeks later to say she'd just cleared the 5-ton minimum capacity for documentation. The big deal for us is that it means she is covered by medical insurance, including liability, hospital, etc. Something the U.S. Public Health Service does for commercial fishermen. So I had to sign a lot of papers, saying, among other things, that I would be loyal to the government in her, not use her trafficking in drugs, bootlegging or whatnot, and that she runs on American made parts, and that her principal use was for commercial mackerel fishing! Mackerel fishing because the Coast Guard recognizes all fishing on this coast as either (1) whaling, and that's illegal; (2) cod fishing, and you're a cod fisherman if you only catch codfish and nothing else; and (3) mackerel fishing.

Officially, then, no other fishing exists here. So all the lobstermen are "mackerel fishermen." "G/S" by the way, means "GAS SCREW." The GAS SCREW ALDA E. Lovely Lady.

Sawyer Young at the saw mill tells of the summer person in summer: Lovely nice here on your coast, but what do they do here in the winter? To which Sawyer Young says: Well in the summertime here, y'see, a lot of fishin' and fuckin'. But in the winter time, not an awful lot of fishin'.

Anyway, there have been a lot of other things to do, despite the hard winter, including dragging lobsters out of the big pound under the ice. Ice fishing. Slim pickins that way. Last month everything was frozen here as far as eye could see, *Seasmoke* smashing ice day in day out, coming everyday like a schoolbus for Sarah and Stephen. Fishermen walking out to their boats in the harbor.

In 1977 Jim bought an old lobster boat. He mused over what to name it, noting that most of the fishermen chose to honor a wife or daughter — Marie Helen, Jenny D., *and* Dorothy E. *all being typical of the harbor fleet. But Jim wanted something else, though he didn't know what. Driving into town one weekend and making the turn at the top of the hill, we slowed as we passed Ivernia's Market. I said "Jim, there it is," pointing at what was left of a SALADA TEA sign glued to the storefront window: AL DA E. Jim arranged the letters on the stern of his boat as they appeared on the window and never told anyone their derivation. Years later he told me someone had recently inquired after his wife, Alda.*

Now mostly gone with wind and tide — storms, though we skate on little pound. Let us know what you decide and maybe we'll come up with small list of desired items. Why not take time off when you get thrown out of apartment and build your house here?

A series of storms here over the past two weeks began with one right on the new moon tide that changed the landscape somewhat. You now have significantly more beachfront at Deep Cove, a beautifully sandy beach heaped up into those alders in the mouth of the brook, and all those biggest spruce trees blown over around the cove including that big one right at the end of your path by the brook and beach — and all that plastic trash driven by the surf way the hell up the brook back into the woods. You won't believe it when you see it. Your view down the brook from your "circle of trees" much more open now — pretty — especially nice your new sandy beach in the mouth of the brook if you clean it up a little — tons of beautiful sand just dumped there! The wind was right southerly, so that your cove would have taken it as hard as anywhere else inside the islands. I'd have loved to be over there watching it pound away — or at Sylvesters' — or can you imagine on the outer cliffs on Monhegan? — 200 feet below like those Irish cliffs. The tide was higher than anyone seems to remember — ever. Rossie's location exposed to that direction, too. He watched his entire wharf go — the whole thing — broke up and drifted off up the gut in huge sections. One (biggest) part ended up on top of Raymond's wharf — logs, spiles, traps still stacked — everything and another section, with traps, landed perfectly situated and level on Ted Coates's ledges, and will probably remain there! Nice little wharf landing for them, without a permit. Rossie's supply of firewood went all adrift — has only odd sticks now — what he can pick up along the beach. His well was swamped by surf (will have to be pumped out in the spring) — so he began going to Raymond's until that last big dump of snow (that you got in the City) — big drift — so now he has had to resort to melting snow for water. Gave Sarah and Stephen each a big glass of Tang the other day from snow-water. Waves pounded right up to Rossie's window, and he watched, then felt pounding on the underside of his floor beneath his feet, huge timbers traveling in surf along the shore, pass right over the wharf, then underneath his house and out the other side! All he lost from that was the corner post underpinning to his south corner. Has a jack under it now. His skiff and outboard were completely swamped and he doesn't intend to try to get the motor fixed again. Too expensive. Bottom and garboards are bad in the skiff. But he's cheerful as ever. Really handsome in white beard. Seems in much better health and spirits than last winter.

Ivan measured eleven inches of water inside his shop (PL. 6), and a mess from floating grease and oil, and a lot of engines and parts on the floor under water. Litterer's white and green boathouse on the other side of the island lost its footing entirely and ended up on the rocks by Crotch Island on its way up the Friendship River. Must have traveled a mile. Joan and I spent our time risking our foolish lives in dory trying to retrieve what began leaving the pound. You can imagine the floating, tossing rubble — including our new dory upside down and drifting off, eight full tanks of propane bobbing off up the gut, dozens of wharf planks

---

Raymond and Florence Cushman's camp is just before Rossie's in the Gut. Raymond was a lobsterman who, I think I am right in saying, never had a driver's license or much interest in straying far from Friendship. Perhaps he saw enough in Europe where he served during World War II. But Raymond was always curious about and often amused by our accounts of life in New York. I remember him standing with one leg up on the stern of his boat, shaking his head in disbelief as I told him about boom boxes, and how kids carried them like big suitcases, their volume pulsing even over the screeching of subway cars. I thought of him years later, after he had died, when his granddaughter, Jennifer (PL. 41), boogied into our clearing one sunny afternoon with a boom box of her own. Once school is out, Florence's grandchildren take turns visiting her on the island. Florence is a natural beauty and as generous as they come. I have run up a big debt with her — easily a dozen berry pies by now.

unpinned and unpinning, two old sections of the weakest part of the fence, cat walk, the runway that leads from the float to the wharf, Post's trash all over everywhere — plastic cans, aluminum boat, barrels, wood, etc. — etc . . . the sea looked like a stew boiling! Stew: our fifty pounds of potatoes and parsnips floating in our cistern-cellar in a mix of sea water and kerosene (from Aladdin lamp we had there for heat, that went adrift). Ripped out that part of wharf that runs right under our west window (PL. 42) (the one planked with 2x3's) — even though I'd tied it down shortly before — the pipe I'd tied it to broke off. Water right up over tops of my boots walking along pound wharf — planks lifting off — dangerous. *Seasmoke* showed up and Boy had me ferry them from the mooring in our dory — one by one (after they'd at first all piled aboard over the side like beachhead invasion and I refused to take them — we'd have swamped for sure. Can you imagine — Boy and 3 like him in dory, and me, in that storm?)....

MARCH 11, 1978

Boy and Popeye got into the turpentine pretty good the other night. (Funny it didn't smell like turpentine.) Came out here to the pound with a "crew" well after dark, the tide arising, to pick up their day's drag of 28 crates of lobsters. Said they had to be shipped out in the morning. Well, I helped them tie them up and close the gate and all, and a gay old time it was — them all to

---

Edward "Boy" Thompson helped Jim with many of his early projects involving hauling and clearing. He was the first Friendship man that I met, and among the nicest and strongest men I have known. Boy came one Sunday morning, after a long Saturday night, to bulldoze alders and stumps at George's. Emmy and Joan were in bathing suits lying in the sun when Boy puffed up the embankment from the cove. Boy surveyed the scene. Amused, mildly astonished, and smiling, he blurted out, "Hey, this ain't bad !" — a line often repeated since that time. Boy worked for Coastal Fisheries, lobstered, and built wharves at various times. He and his family lived a couple of years at the lobster pound on Long Island.

be down to the island working at that hour, as you can maybe imagine. Steve set out ahead in the skiff towing the crates up the Gut in the dark until the rest caught up with him, out in the bay well beyond Bald Rock, to transfer the tow lines to the *Seasmoke*. I could see by her lights that she'd stopped out there and could hear them talking and knocking things around on the steel deck, and then after a while was surprised to see her heading off towards Dix Point, but a while later she had turned and was steaming back in towards the harbor and I went in and went back to bed.

Well, details of the event are not entirely clear, but these are they, more or less, filtered back here to the island. Boy tends to run his ship less by the book and more by his own instincts. And so, out there in the bay that night, the transfer of tow lines completed, and with running lights all ablaze and cheerful, he threw her into reverse to go forward and (as Ross would say) then he give it to her. Well, the crates, of course, were all tied up taut right behind her, and that obedient old *Seasmoke* propeller, churning back around like some kind of meat grinder, just sucked everything in under the stern. Wound up lines around the shaft, cut them, smashed things up in good shape — and generally managed to ship most of those lobsters out earlier than planned. What they didn't grind up they freed up, and those crates that were still intact were set adrift into the black of night with little hope (or will) of recovery. In the morning the crated ones were found frozen dead, left on the beach by the tide. The rest may very well get Delbert out here with his traps a little early this spring. Seems to have pretty good luck lobstering around the pound.

_____

MAY 2, 1978

I can't get past May 1st any more without thinking of early mornings along the river with Dave Haller. Scanning pastures, hobbling, uttering — like some bird call of his own: Hey-hey! It's the first of May. Outdoor frigging begins today. Big sun behind those spindly trees on the island east of the cornfield. And tells how the look of the May trees always reminds him of Frost: Nature's first green is gold.

Well, the eider ducks here in the bay, the gut, the cove, have been outdoors frigging since about the middle of March. Pretty soon now the flashy males, young swains, will once again flee to the outer-islands and leave the ladies to their nests, and by the time you all arrive, those tiny trails of duck families will be paddling around the shore like Michael in the kayak. We've been having something of a spring drought here — wonderful days of sun and dry breezes — and have been taking advantage. Work on the boat — burning paint and puttying and painting, and we've got some things in the garden weeks earlier than the usual spring bog will permit. Some nice visits with Harold Benner, who is building a skiff for the Borsts. I had a chance to share a day's rent, very cheap, of a pneumatic drill and so got all my holes (partially) dug for the concrete posts upon which the New George's place will rest. And then, on low water, went down to Deep Cove and drilled holes in ledges in which to anchor offhauls — for you and for us. Good spots, I think.

_____

OCTOBER 31, 1978

Halloween morning, wonderful, clear sky — not cold, strong S-W chop, windy, glorious. Eve of All Saints, but the saints here must be scallops — the season opens tomorrow. Fondling my dip-net already. The way the native hunters ride around in their pickups with their rifles in the rear windows, anticipating the deer. . . .

Two week gap in this. So much to tell, though. So much to do. My father coming. We're still in the cottage, big old black iron cookstove — a "Star Kineo" 1910 model, made in Bangor — set in front of the fireplace, keeping warm. We love the stove, a real

_____

Michael Borst is a multi-talented artist and carpenter who lives in Oxford, England. He was formerly married to Deborah Macy (Pratt), an architect and exquisite draftsman, whose family has summered on the island for several decades. One winter Michael stayed in Florence Cushman's camp where he worked on small sculptures and helped Jim work at George's.

cooker — a monument, an altar. The old-timers' equivalent of the TV set, no doubt. Will be lovely moved out to George's. A slow steady heat. Probably next month we will move out there for the deep part of winter, then in March back to here so we can tear the lid off the place out there for the new building. Seems somehow backwards, doesn't it? — moving onto the island to keep warm (in a very temporary, black paper and scrap-lumber wing — solar exposed, greenhouse-like, on the sunny side-addition, very temporary, to the old homey quarters) and onto the mainland in the spring. Besides, the other 2/3 of the management here are rattling a lot of sabres about getting our posteriors out of this place afraid we're going to burn the place down, because we don't know 'nawthin'. Ranks and pecking orders and a lot of rationalizations — the same old story. Hell . . . you can't fire me! I quit!

Which is what, more or less, happened at the pound. Not long after you were here, the boss girded up his loins — which are considerable — and hustled out to Little Island to deliver us our two weeks' notice. Literally. Lock stock and barrel. Kit and kaboodle, bag and baggage. Two weeks. Like that. "I need somebody that's going to work." The rest of the story is too ugly to tell here. Other than to say that it soon became clear that the god - father behind the whole adventure was not Johnny but Post himself — it seems incredible, but it's true. You are right. "Crazy" was your word. . . .

And so we seem to be alone again, and unemployed, and cellar full of vegetables. And happier. But what is it that seems to want to kick us out of places? Tinker's blood. Or it may be them reading down to my own secret wish to be gone. . . .

Wonderful halfmoon tonight on powder snow. Dead quiet. The whole world shades of blue-black — except for light out our windows — even the white is blue-black. Stars big as buttons.

November 24, 1978

A nice Thanksgiving, on the island. My father didn't come, either, it turned out. So we cleaned things out of George's, laid the little red oriental rug over the plywood and put out the table for Ivan and Jose. A full house — Lovan on the bed, and on the floor eating turkey skin. A kind of repeat of four years ago, and symbolic in a way of our return there. Jose brought over a buttercup squash pie, and Toby. Then late in the afternoon Joan and Sarah made up a big pie-plate of a little of everything. TV-dinner style — foil on the top and took it over to Ross. Sarah's own mince pie, Joan's stuffing that had our own Jerusalem artichokes in it, like water chestnuts. A turnip from the garden sweet as honey — been through a lot of freezes — we still haven't pulled them yet — frost sweetens them, and the parsnips, too. The day prior to the dinner we acquired five lovely old chairs from Delbert — his house on the island. We've needed them, nice old wooden chairs, from the beginning out there — really add a lot to the place, including comfort. A chair for Ross but he of course wouldn't come — "now ain't that quee-ah — I don't eat out" — you remember. But on his birthday we all, at his place, had a bite of chocolate jelly roll cake Sarah baked for him. Couldn't come up with the 81 candles but he blew out what we had. No wish — said he forgot, when Stephen asked. His health seems very good — walks over to call on us often twice a day lately, even in bad weather. Earlier in the year he'd go for weeks without getting out — corns were bothering him a lot, and then that cough. Ivan and Jose seem as well as ever — she taking a lot of bone meal to help her joints and Ivan

---

Ivan and Josephine Morse were the true islanders, living there year round for more than twenty years — alone most of those winters. Ivan had a mechanic's shop on his wharf and worked on boats, engines, and tools. Art Spear, who lives on Davis Point, transcribed and edited Ivan's wonderful oral history, Friendship Long Island. Josephine gardened, kept chickens, braided rugs, and helped with all the requirements of island living. And she was not afraid to confront clammers who had the temerity to dig up her beach, legally or not. Josephine was proud and dignified. She had severe arthritis in her fingers and I remember seeing her modestly tuck her hands into the folds of her dress when I photographed her (Pl. 7). Jim and Joan were grateful to Ivan and Josephine for their advice in those first years on the island. Ivan and Josephine have both died and are buried in the island cemetery.

grimly cheerful, feeling he's failing, not good for very much any more — when he remembered how easily he used to shoulder a sack of corn from the shore to the house for the hens. They got very little from their garden this year — so dry. They both looked so nice for the dinner — Josephine in a lovely quite old purple knit long dress, and showing us her double-lined red mittens from Switzerland. Said she didn't know why Ivan didn't freeze coming over in just his sweater. They were both worried about Toby these last few nights — hadn't come home to sleep and it being so cold. Just coming around a little bit in the daytime now. They wondered whether maybe some folks had come on the island for a few days. There have been deer hunters around. Ronald shot a small deer that Jose was watching feed in her orchard the other day.

Albert told me he and Ronald were planning to bring a coon dog onto the island one night last week for a coon hunt — $25 a pelt. I told him I hoped they would for our garden's sake. He caught 5 in all this year, and all before any'd gotten to the corn. Corn coming out of our ears, so to speak, till long after you were gone — longest corn crop ever this year, by far. The entire garden, in fact — except for the pumpkins — was best one yet, by far. Good luck right from the beginning. When dry spring allowed us to plant earlier than usual. Luckiest thing, of course, was the well that never went dry, the pitcher pump right in the garden. Can you believe the drought worsens still? Late November? Many wells have been dry for weeks, even longer, others drying up every day — all around the state, certain parts. Ours at the cottage has gone very salty (though less so than sea water itself) because of the low level. When spring water drains out of the fissures in rock, the salt water presses in to replace it. Walking around tasting the salt in my teeth these days — tooth brushing, and in the orange juice we make, the powdered milk, etc. Now the authorities are worried that the ground will freeze before we get any substantial rain, or melted snow on the ground. If that happens, then the water that eventually comes will simply run off without seeping into the lower level to replenish the wells. Could be bad. Seems like one of the plagues out of the Old Testament. A lot of people lugging water from wherever they can get it, I hear. We've been lucky. And George's place a kind of oasis, a garden (PL. 4).

APRIL 30, 1979

"Life is a journey from nowhere to nowhere . . ." upside down through apple trees head-on into the hillside. Post crashed last Friday. Was attempting to land on a tail wind on a gravel airstrip in Jonesboro, down east. Picture of the plane — on "grassy knoll" — in the Bangor paper, familiar, even if dismembered. He had left here on Wednesday with a woman. "It's great to be young. Haw! And if you can't be young you can at least be foolish." Journey from nowhere to Jonesboro. God bless him. Didn't even have his dog with him. What will become of the island?

Ivan is in the hospital — collapsed behind his grocery cart in Ted's Save-More Supermarket. We and others have been getting Josephine to and from the hospital, on and off the island. She dresses up in light blue every day — hat and coat. Last week walking with her to the beach I said: How are you, Jose? Good, she said. I have to be. They seem to have gotten his heart steadied up but think he might have other problems — ulcer, maybe gall bladder. Not sure. They're taking a lot of x-rays. Ivan told us Thursday he was feeling better. "Better than them that have to take care of me." Is short of strength. There's no telling when he'll be home. Enjoyable visits with him. As you can imagine. Josephine is worried, tired — stays as long as she can with him every day. She treated us to reuben sandwiches at the hospital cafeteria the other day. The hospital is Pen-Bay, the new one in Rockport, that Mrs. Wescott left a million dollars to, to have built. Years ago Paul Wescott had given his friend Wyeth a painting he'd done of Ivan's house — view from the rear looking out across the cove — small figure of Josephine standing by the back door. Called the painting "Mary's House" (Mary Davis, Ivan's ancestor). Wyeth later gave it to the hospital in Westcott's honor. Ivan's room is right around the corner from where it hangs.

When Ivan collapsed in Ted's Save-More they had the ambulance right there. It happened that another old fellow, also in the market, had collapsed at about the same time, of similar ailment. Signs of the Apocalypse. I don't know whether they saved more or not, but they loaded the two of them right in together, cheek by jowl — double bagged, I imagine — for the hospital. . . .

Yes, and even a god damned earthquake. Dark of night, distant muffled thunder-rumble. Rolled Bill Hall out of sleep and heading for the cellar — told Evelyn the furnace had blown up. I'd thought it was an airplane but then it went on too long — stood listening to it outside next to the rattling gas hood, Joan thought she could see the house shaking. Quake was centered near Bath. Technicians inside the Maine Yankee Nuclear Plant in Wiscasset reported to the news folks the next day that they "hadn't felt a thing." Still, you have to imagine that the Clamshell Alliance was responsible for the whole thing. Somehow. Did you know that only just last fall Ted Coates had made me the Civil Defense Director, complete with epaulets for the island? Rossie failed to show for the muster on Raymond's wharf. Raymond said he can remember as a small boy an earthquake breaking dishes in the pantry. Every which way but loose.

It failed, however, to topple your shed. A few more trees have been brought down, though, since your departure — by unnatural causes. We opened up the double maple by the brook (the morning sun seems to ascend right through it) and burned both piles without including the house. Some of the bottom of that pile we could not move because of frost — still — believe it or not. (Last week we walked up through Back Bone with Ross to the schoolhouse — to look for the old spring — and crossed a broad patch of ice on the road ledge.) Joan and I have been saving up 18 foot timbers — lumber for the house — out of your logs, but haven't moved anything out yet. Place still looks like a battlefield, sun striking down on bodies fallen every which direction. We'll try to get it cleared up some before you come so you'll have a bit of space to move around in. Rossie marvels over the cordage of

Bill and Evelyn Hall own and operate the gas wharf at the end of the harbor. They sell gas, oil, and Milky Ways to fishermen and boaters year round. UPS and practically everyone else leaves packages, deliveries, and messages for island folks with them. The mastlike rigging above their wharf office is for a radio antenna that allows Bill, a devoted ham operator, to speak to people all over the world. He and Evelyn have been providing such indispensable service and kindness for so long that there is a tendency to take them for granted.

wood in that small area — will pay us a hundred bucks next fall for two cords delivered. He wants to buy my McCulloch but we'll cut it up for him and split it once to dry. Got to build a stone bridge across your brook. Much to do.

Sawmill works wonderfully. We cut those big hackmatack on our Little Field road and sawed them up into 6x6's for sills — got them all finished some time ago and hauled out of the woods — one was over 28 feet long, another 32, others 18 and shorter, down to 8 feet. They'll be super. George Simmons tells us the old timers used hackmatack under the cows' feet, in stalls — hard core it has, and won't rot. Beautiful grain. Think we'll saw some up into boards later on to use as flooring. Or if we're lucky we might dismantle some from an old barn around. Seal up the seams here with old cowflops.

We've lately knocked off work on the new George's because of a reversal of schedule: Delbert's fish house is to be moved May 12th, a Saturday — so we've had to do a lot for that — preparation. Here's what's happened. We've contracted Roland Bragg from Nobleboro, housemover, to engineer the whole thing — going to do it all in one day, one tide — if all goes well — with a crew. And ALDA E. Joan and I are doing a lot of preparatory work — sawing up 12 18' logs into 5x5 timbers (on the sides only) to be used as rails to roll the building on, driving pins into the ledge both on Delbert's beach and on Flat Rock Beach, constructing a log and rail system fastened to Flat Rock Beach to serve as cradle to set the floating building down on, reinforcing the building somewhat so that it will withstand the move — even helping Delbert clear all his stuff out (they came for the herring nets last week — still have the ones in the loft to remove) — and transporting some of Bragg's equipment out to the island ahead of time, on high tide. It's going to be very simple, really. Bragg has, by chance, two 24' aluminum tanks — old military aircraft refueling tanks he's only used once before — he's going to make a kind of sling out of them — a tank either side of the building, joined together under the floor with cables — and with jacking, blocking, pipe rollers and our rails from your logs will set the building down on the beach and let the tide carry it off. (Guided by the ALDA E.) Giant water wings. Maybe some styrofoam fore and aft for stability. Then on Flat Rock Beach we will reverse steps and set the building, as the tide leaves, Sat. afternoon, right where we want it — a little higher in elevation so we'll be able, Joan and I, to construct the piling system underneath — then set the building down on it — on our own time. The whole project hangs on the weather. But we have a good run of tides coming if we do have to wait a day or two.

Well, we're very excited about it — want very much for you to be here for the picnic. Clambake. Hoe down. Seems to be a primitive event somehow. A rite you might read about in the Golden Bough. Mountain moving. Some such thing — a rite of passage. Slaughter and transport to the tribe — of elephant to Pygmy village. Dancing and feasting and merriment. Full moon nights, in May.

JANUARY 28, 1980

Enjoying thoughts about your letters, and of course the photographs on the obverse. Do we owe Daniel Wolf something for them? It's truly wonderful news, your contract with the gallery.

The sole dealers of your work. And of our own lawn here, to "notable collectors" — our lovely green ass immortalized, taken away — when what we really need is for somebody to take away pieces of the trash on the other side of the house . . . is what is meant by the prostitution of one's art, by golly. It feels terrific!

The "sole dealers" around here — by the "fillet-of" — have kind of gone out of business, it would seem. Including Lloyd and and his fish truck. He's gone to scalloping with Blaine Davis lately. The price of ground fish being so low — it's ridiculous — the fish never so plentiful, the fishermen so willing — but reluctant to go out, for the price. The folks who are making a worthwhile profit, they say, are the big "fish factory" ships way out on the banks — put the little guys right out of the market. Basic food, all around — fish, delicious, mild, needing only to be gathered up — and they can't, or won't go. Seems like living in a field of blueberries in July the ground purple all around you, and they tell you it wouldn't be worth your time to pick them. They're bedfellows

with the grain farmers, I think.

No market for lobsters now, I hear — presumably because of "recession" — lobster priced right out of reach. And what with the steady, ever-present dull roar of the winter wind, no one is heading out of the harbor any more. And of course the price of fuel. No VW Rabbits in those bilges you know. In short the air is silent of engine, astir with steady chop, with the spray from "white feathers" — freezing instantly on contact, and with wavering, subway roar of spruce. Clean, though — everything is. The rockweed, frozen, is frosted and crushes underfoot to the offhaul, mornings, and stays in place. You can run on it safely — like that stiff grey lichen underfoot in the summer. And the mudslop in the cove — you walk on its surface, stiff as frozen chocolate pie. I picked up mussels out there the other day — They were marvelous — best I think I've had. Thought of course of you — you'd have to say whether these are better than in the summer. Don't know why that would be, but . . . seemed so to me. Fleshy. Sweet and mild. We had them before a batch of Saturday night baked beans and cornbread. And moon on the snow behind the garden. Sarah baked an apple crisp. The house is banked this year all around with hay and so we are living in a nest. The constant presence of the wind seems, in here, even friendly — renders it cozier, nestier. As though we're almost in the spruce trees those big towering ones beside the house, that dwarf us (PL. 2). Static in summer — but so alive now, in motion, slow, ponderous circles that their spines make when you look towards the tops. They dwarf us, and are of course ever threatening, especially as you lie awake on a brutal night, listening to the stove, to the cats in the cellar among the potatoes and things, and to the NW wind. Kind of like living for a while in one of those little Christmas creche structures, fragile, tentative, focused in on itself. The bright lamps through the windows at night (outside for a minute in your undershirt to take a piss). The warm air — invisible curtain — when you open the door again, the warm commotion — Sarah and Stephen stretched out on the floor, inching out a labyrinth of dominoes in our cavernous new room. You should see us, rattling around in here now — seems sometimes you can barely see from one end of the room to the other — will get lost looking for my drink when the spring fogs come. It's actually only a 10'x8' extension on the one room — we simply moved that windowed wall out to the new sills you remember, and added a window on the SE side for more sun, and then closed everything in very temporarily for the winter so that it will dismantle easily after the new building proper is built around it. Still, small as it is, it makes a whopping 60% larger house for us than previous winters — still not a stitch of insulation, and still easy to heat with just the cook stove (having a relatively small firebox). We translated Sarah and Stephen into the new wing, rope-beds and all (bunks lower now, with plenty of headroom for doing homework on haunches) and added a lamp by the big windows. And so that entire end of things is totally theirs now and we're all just delighted.

Tiny a step forward as this little addition is, the construction is at a stage now where the whole rest of the house can be built right while we are living here — having assembled the present tacked-together wing in such a way as not to interfere with the new work. Certain critical, anxiety-producing things (to the old place) are already behind us — such as tearing a 14' gaping hole in the roof and cutting through rafters, studs, plate, etc., and setting up — through the old roof — three of the new 6x6 posts — 11 footers, sawed up this fall from your logs (PL. 53) that are the backbone of the new east wall. They required a lot of fussing and fitting to the everywhichway old building — but have turned out better than I ever could have imagined — a lot of luck in fact, in so many ways. But it's all encouraging, so far, and can't wait to get started in earnest once again as soon as the days permit. There are hazards in this method (of building new house around old, right while inhabiting — in winter — on island): one big blow of overnight SE wind took the black paper roof-hole cover clean off — back in that warm spell and by the time I got out here afterwards it had rained right in, roof-runoff and all — all over everything (almost), the house was in puddles — rugs soaked — papers, table, wall — even the cats looked wet. But it could have been a lot worse (such as it all then suddenly freezing solid) and we are now dry — and washed! — and roof sealed up with a new piece of paper, and caulked around the jutting posts. The paper is such a thin roof that the cats frequently climb up

there at night and sit on it for the radiating stove heat. Worries me sometimes — that one night soon one of them will suddenly burst in, like Santa Claus. At times, it's kind of like wintering in a bombed-out teepee.

I've been doing a lot of head-work — planning, visualizing, dozing — at night while the rest are asleep, as I have to get up every few hours for the stove — what with little hardwood in our pile and a small firebox. Catnapping — catch as catch can — and mostly enjoying it. These long nights of wind and bright moon, and snow. Been thinking of you, in fact, getting up for 2 o'clock feedings and all that — stoking up the baby, feeding the stove. I remember Joan read a lot of books in those days. At worst, it's tolerable because it's temporary, and I nurture fantasies of March, when baby will have learned to sleep through again.

FEBRUARY 4, 1980

A gap. We're back at the Cadys' now, for another week — then back to the Armstrongs' till spring. Davis Pt. house hopping, the circle tour. The ice was a real threat on groundhog's day — broken up, massive cakes piling up into the harbor ahead of 45 mph southerly winds. The painter on our boat pulled taut as a steel rod — but held. Many other boats weren't so fortunate. Some parted their moorings, others simply dragged, moving with the icebergs — and started out across the harbor in the morning with the shift in the wind to westerly. A lot of rain, and salt water leaking in besides — and then sudden drop in temperature — a mess. But you've got to cope with it — day by day go out and pump — bail, chip ice — watch the wind, all but helplessly. The *Seasmoke* has been delivering fishermen to their boats — as we can't walk anymore and it's next to impossible to get a skiff through the floes. We've been doing pretty well with the dory, though the *Seasmoke* churned up a path yesterday ahead of us so we could get back to the wharf. February is the "ice month" here (as the water is so cold) and we have another month of this to look forward to. Last year it didn't freeze up till March. One of our windshields blew off the ALDA E weeks ago and plastic doesn't last long. Snow goes everywhere. The float on the end of the town wharf has buckled and torn apart (from pressure of ice and tides). Bill Hall's float is tilted and partially submerged — unbalancing the inner ears of ducks — a middle section of John Armstrong's (Cady's) wharf has heaved and collapsed. Ice along the shore is up to 3 feet thick, and underneath most of the wharves the ice is right solid — beach to high water mark — constantly working, of course, with the tide heaving upwards owing to its buoyancy.

Every day since the ice broke up Joan and I have been hopeful of getting out to see Ross and to check on things. But each time have failed — some clog or other prevents it every day — though each day's ice pattern is different. Anxious to see the fishhouse and the building we left at George's. And Ross. His niece made him a stew we promised to deliver — keep taking it out of the freezer, hopefully, and returning it. And lugging back and forth to the boat a jar of the applesauce he likes, and mail.

Enough of this ice — this winter. This talk-wearisome weather.

Joan and I hitched a ride with a neighbor last week to Rockland to pick up the bus. Back seat of something — new, small — maybe a Saab. Heater on, went probably half a mile, and you know what — panicked. She had to stop the car. I thought I was going to bust through the window. So scary. Crazy. It's physical. Things blur — weightless sensation — heart pumping, short of breath. I could barely ask her to stop. Stammering. Joan, sitting beside me, said she didn't know what was happening. Everybody was very nice about it. (What is epilepsy?) I was so surprised. It hadn't happened like that since the back seat of Cary Bell's VW bug, rainy night, coming home from a play at the Stage Company, probably ten years ago. One forgets.

Ken Cady is a retired naval officer who now lives on Davis Point with his wife, Mary. Ken still keeps everything from his khaki pants to his flowering bushes ship-shape. Their son, Sam Cady, is a friend and painter whose work was included in the recent exhibition and book, On the Edge: Forty Years of Maine Painting.

Part of the panic, for me, I think, is being somehow unable, physically, to ask the driver to stop the car — speechless panic — the stammering thing. Body's need to break out getting ahead of the brain's — mouth's — function of structuring words — to bring about the need's wish — to break out (of what?).

Probably having something to do with dumping 10 pages of them here onto you. Words — seeing their own shadow — busting through 6 more weeks of winter.

I sighted an eagle the other day — the first one ever that I know of — hanging over the cover, the ice. The biggest bird I have ever seen, by far — awesome — it looked almost too heavy to be in the air. It was late in the day, white broad underwings in a gray sky. All the associations, the symbolism, ever attached to eagles are justified.

APRIL 16, 1980

Indeed the landscape is changing. Been thinking how you'd better get back here before they move the island out from under. Ifemey has sold out to Atwood Bros., who own several places round about. They plan to turn it into a seafood takeout. Downeast Airlines is dissolving next month. The FAA report on last year's fatal crash at Owl's Head is damning of the DE management — cited for putting undue pressure on its pilots to fly when they should not. Bar Harbor Airlines is taking over the flights to Boston. Even the Thorndike has a new face, and innards. It's opened as a little "mall" of Camden-like shops — wine and cheese, handicrafts, a deli in the back. A federal report issued yesterday and endorsed by Sen. Muskie finds significant increases recently in tidal pollution, resulting in, among other things, a reduction in the soft shell clam population. The Maine Dept. of Environmental Protection last week issued its permit to Martin Marietta, the Thomaston cement plant, to switch over to coal fired energy. The plant promptly announced that they plan to emit air pollutants to the highest level allowable by law. And so with the coal stacks to the east and Wiscasset to the west, this island declares itself hopelessly affixed to the spiritual life of the Great

North American Continent. Then last week's news of monitoring the drinking water in Brunswick and Sanford, for carcinogenic chemical traces, and advising folks not to take alarm . . . because if 100,000 citizens drank the water for 75 years, then not one in . . . would die of. . . .

These are days of grace now — between the deep freeze and the mosquitoes. March's lion this year brought with him the first total freeze-up of harbor and bay. Plague of ice, plague of wind — the visitations. They are winter's translations of the summer plagues, of mosquitoes and of fog. But the days are long now and the birds seeming all to come back at once — first the geese — the high honks of around 30 of them I watched from in front of your shed. And what must have been your owl a few days later while I was sawing lumber — swooped along the back edge of your clearing and into the woods. And this week your friends the vipers, two of them — one under a log at Back Bone and one by the granite foundation of Ted's grandfather's house. I ordinarily won't see two in a whole year. Meaning you'll likely be stepping on two hundred. A sign, I believe, of the Apocalypse. Was somewhere writ.

MAY 2, 1980

Bernard Wallace went to sea the other day, for lobsters. Not a breath of wind, but out off Allen's Head where he was there were swells — you know how it is — calm nights after previous storms you can hear the steady roar of swells — no wind, no chop

---

Bernard and Marie Wallace lived summers on the island for years. They still come out Sundays to look after things. Bernard's lobster boat, Marie Helen, *his buoys, the wharf, their houses, and the grounds are all immaculate. Marie rides her mower over a rolling clovered lawn that looks like a golf green. Their dog Rosie oversees everything, though she now has difficulty climbing the wharf ladder she used to scamper up. Time and chance happen to us all. Bernard has always struck me as a man of deep feeling.*

breaking on the shore of the outer islands. Bernard drove his boat in towards the shore to haul one of his traps, turned her side-to, and a giant swell suddenly broke right next to him — broke in fact right over the top of his canopy! Smashing it, and drenched his engine — and himself. And of course crippling the boat. The next swell that came along carried everything — boat and Bernard — high up on the shore. Just this side of the cliffs of Allen's Head. (If it had been cliffs and not shore, that would have been the whole ballgame.) The boat, miraculously, got a hole or two in the hull and a scarred keel and not much else other than the smashed canopy — a strong boat. Bernard injured a knee, and was of course soaked to the skin — thought he was going to freeze to death — stood around as much as two hours before they found him and got him off. Couldn't get on the C.B. We saw the little flotilla going by late in the morning — of rescuers. Coast Guard with Bernard's boat lashed alongside, and Buddy, Allen Simmons, Albert, and others who pulled him off. Bernard seems ok now and the boat about to be launched — next week.

A few days later some of the more ambitious fishermen — Donald (the younger), Peter Murphy — and brother and father — son and grandsons of Wilbur, of ALDA E history — and Preston Carter went out early to fish their halibut trawls — to the Caches Ledge twenty-five-odd miles out, far past Monhegan — wind calm or light — good weather predicted. When they do that, they usually anchor overnight and stay two or three days out there. Next day a NE wind started up. Strong — unpredicted till it had arrived (we noticed it that way ourselves, following the reports) — a gale in fact. They figured up to 50 mph. Seas as big as a house. They rode out the night as best they could. All of them ultimately losing their anchors — in the morning started out in a group — behind a 57-foot scalloper from Owls Head in the lead for Provincetown — Mass. That being the only direction they could go. Scared as hell. Even the scalloper was in trouble. Was a ten-hour trip — but they all made it. Called up Mrs. Murphy: "Hi, Mom. We're in Provincetown." The big danger in going with the wind — a "following sea" — is that the boat can become a surf board, riding down the lead side of the huge waves and end up ass over teakettle in the one ahead. Loop-de-loop. Roly wholly over. On the way back to Friendship, returning to the trawls they set, they found eight nice halibut on the hook — one a monster — 164 lbs. A good price for halibut, too, a delicacy. Jonathan said the catch just about paid for the gas.

Signs and wonders. Toby has had a haircut. Trim and thin. It took 3 men to anchor him and one to clip. Violent crime is up. Witnessed four mallard drakes on a hen the other day on Bill Hall's front lawn! We've been getting eggs. They're excellent in cakes. Boy is back, it seems, at work for the Coastal Fisheries. Plus ça change, plus c'est la meme chose.

MAY 8, 1980

Johnny Neubig has bought a farm just outside the village, on the road to East Friendship. Big old house, barn, land right down to the back river — fields, pasture, garden. Nice. They've been tearing it all apart, fixing it up. Expect one day to have a "critter" in the pasture, Johnny says. He didn't build a new boat this winter, as planned — "for somethin' t' do." Bought a farm instead.

But Albert the Fire Chief, together with the Benner boys, Wayne and Arnold, did buy a boat — went downeast for her and drove her back, and now have got her all fitted out — all rigged up for ground fishing. They've been going out for a month or two now, and if it works out they intend to sell their lobster boats and carry on with the ground fish. I hope it does. One boat, three men together instead of three separate boats — lobstering is expensive and wasteful business in so many ways — this would seem to make sense. Others are getting into it, too. The boat has been documented in the name of Miss Dolly. You will remember the

---

Albert Simmons is a fisherman and the Fire Chief. His friendly manner, burly build, and full reddish beard make him hard to miss. As an outsider, it is hard to know, but Albert seems to be one of the people that gives stability and balance to the Friendship community. He and Ronnie Simmons (no relation) often hunt together on the island.

poster last summer in Albert's pilot house? Seems safer these days, instead of naming your boat after some wife or other.

Joan's got the peas in already. Usually ours get caught in the summer heat and don't do well (peas like it cool) and so we thought we'd try some higher in the (drier) garden. The old timers' goal for pea planting was the 17th of March — green for St. Patrick.

JANUARY 2, 1981

Anyhow, I am pretty thoroughly disentangled, emotionally, from ambitions with the house, the construction — happy to let it sit for 3 months — and write. I have evacuated all but a few of my notorious notes from the island and am kind of filled with their old ghosts already. In fresh clothes, alive and breathing deep, and growing onto the page. I'm 40 years old in two months, and that's old. A year for getting off ass. Welcome the winter — but it's still a shock to stay indoors. I keep looking out at the water. Ice. Go down and pump out the boat. Worry a little.

JANUARY 30, 1981

We have been frozen up solid here since New Year's. The

Johnny Neubig fished on his boat, Three D's, *and worked as a mason until multiple sclerosis slowed him down. He has a camp (PL. 23) on the shore beyond Deep Cove. He stacked his traps there and on Sundays he would come out to dig clams, fix a plank, chat. With his curiosity and native intelligence, Johnny seems to know something about almost everything. After he came down with MS, he worked half days and built us a fine chimney and hearth. It meant a lot to me and Emmy to see his work become part of the house, and we were touched by his interest and courage. Johnny and his wife, Janet, have two sons, David and Dwayne. David (PL. 50) has been lobstering for several years on his own boat, the* Salty Cod, *and Dwayne works for Bath Iron Works.*

boats' positions fixed as in a photograph — west southwest. A boat always seems to leak more in the wintertime and ours is no exception. Ours has been so slow that the water freezes in the bilge pretty much as fast as it leaks in — so we finally had to start in with the salt and hatchet and hammer — and on a warm day hot water in a bucket to thaw out the bilge pump. The heavy ice lasted until the very end of the week's "thaw" and we had been walking right out to work on the boat. But Thursday all the boats got broken out, and so now we row out to work — when the ice goes it goes all of a sudden. Scary. There is still a great cap of heavy ice across the head of the cove that in a NE wind could let go and take everything with it. The best you can do is get out ahead of it or duck in behind the wharf as it passes. Boats have been known to vanish overnight without a trace — or, if your mooring is good, your boat could be pulled right under as the ice passes overhead. Eaton Davis is going to give us a call if he sees it coming.

The ice is kind of fun if you don't have to worry about it. We skied three times out to the island (it's quite a long walk to George's by water — a long flat field to cross) and called on Ross. He is well — remarkably cheerful — we got him a couple of buckets of water from his well. There is no ice on the well surface, suprisingly — for all this sub-zero cold there has been enough snow to insulate. Water level is high — we dipped down by hand to fill his bucket. Two weeks ago Ross was visited by no less than seventeen snowmobiles — a club outing, the "Stormy Riders Snowmobile Club," including Johnny and Janet Neubig. They seemed to appear from the mouth of the Friendship River, zipped around the point on Garrison for a muster by the black buoy, then took off in a long caravan for Litterer's point and their island tour. It was great. We were at George's door when they passed — some of them — behind the garden from Arthur's hill — it seemed like a freight train going through. Stormy Riders. Marlboro Country.

The first of the times we skied to the island bitter cold, windy afternoon — we crossed from Davis Pt. to Litterer's Wharf, stepping gingerly, the wind at our backs. The sensation was really marvelous, the waters underfoot, tamed at last — unshifting, im-mobile — solid state. This is the first winter in seven that we've been able to walk home. While on the island, sheltered somewhat, we could hear the wind stiffen and a snow squall breezed up. Fine, pelting flakes — and it was getting on towards dusk when, having left Ross's, we came out of the Litterers' woods for the return crossing and to see what it was out there, these sounds — strange, muffled gnash and rumble, a pounding behind the mind. A ship — Coast Guard stripes, an ice breaker — was plowing up the harbor! Seen only as a gray hulk at first, enormous. Flat image through a haze of blowing snow, steaming straight up the channel. It looked like an ocean liner, gone to see Bill Hall — a battleship. Weird heavy pounding, the curl of ice thrown up by her bow, barely, dully heard — a dream shadow — the whole situation, our situation. Bergman, *The Seventh Seal*: Death works his bucksaw at the base of the tree, far below, wherein I perch . . . and so rushed out onto the ice towards it, waving our arms. Desert survivors flagging down aircraft miles away. Gray light of day, and failing, the ship heading out past the spindle, Ram Island, Gull Rock . . . the curvature of the earth across a mile — a shadow, blurring. I said to Joan, Maybe it'll come back. The ice ends before Wreck Island.

And eventually it did — shadow growing larger almost as if willed there by us — we hadn't really expected it to. By then we had skied nearer to the scar of its wake through the ice, towards the center of the harbor. And became aware of a voice, a hollering down the wind, repeating . . . a man in an orange jacket standing on the end of the company wharf: Hey! Hey . . . ! waving his arms — go back! You can't get off the island! Telling us the ship had been through (it was on its way back by now). We shouted back — I can't remember what — against the wind, unintelligible, surely — voices across a field of ice, like echoes. And him resuming, frustrated, Hey — ! Townsfolk had us on the C.B., we were told later — two or three in cars even came to watch, from Clem's hill. Someone thought they might even have radioed the ship. A quarter mile away now — we way out on the ice, standing, waiting, as for a bus — they had to see us now. And did. Slowed. Stopped dead in the ice — no bow wave, no tremor, no sound even of the engines — as though itself suddenly frozen in the ice, as in those old photographs of Labrador whalers. Two crewmen came out, down from the bridge to the bow rail, called to us — waved to us to keep going up the harbor, to the black buoy. Then we understood. The ship hadn't gone through past Garrison and the bay, had gone only up as far as the clam factory and turned around, intending to break out only the western side of the island. The orange man had feared the worst, as we had, and we could hear him and the Coast Guard hollering back and forth as the ship plowed by his point of vantage once again. Nearly dark now. We met Dick near the black buoy, pulling his canoe across behind him, heading home to the pound like a Husky with a sled. Had a great laugh together — laughed over details — Ha! — Such laughing as after a dream of cold drowning. Slipping through ice, walking off the edge of the earth. Joan was cold. Stephen was coping with adventure, and I was — felt — crazy with resolution. Luck, bad and good, had converged in an hour to work itself out. Wondering what us God damn fools might conjure up for tomorrow. Some new exhilarating terror.

<hr>

APRIL 22, 1981

Because of our relatively early spring we've been able to get some things in the garden already: peas, lettuce, carrots, spinach — even a long row of early red potatoes! We're optimistic. It's wonderful to be working the soil once again. Rich, light compost from last year's garbage. Rhubarb and asparagus are up — and we're eating wintered-over parsley and chives. Labo rolls in the sunny dirt and in her clump of catnip. Raymond's tree swallows are back — 6 days earlier on the calendar this year than last. Inspecting our boxes. Maybe yours — ?

You have at least 2 rows of lettuce! The size of alfalfa sprouts. Deep rich green little buds — to go with your expanse of lawn. They're as thick as sprouts in a jar, too — and we'll have to thin (eat) them for you before the bunnies do. Your garden! what excitement. Your peonies look great — a lot of maroon buds poking up in the sun. Your fallen tree even righted itself mostly — thawed at the stump. Place looks wonderful. Piles gone. Brighter for the trees taken.

JANUARY 9, 1982

I am sorry to be so long gone. We think of you often, your letter, thinking to answer it on the back of a photograph of my office at George's Place but I couldn't get a word in edgewise. Even on the backside, in the backhouse. All that clutter. Where is your clutter? Low sunlight in a jar of honey, on white. Clear. Mr. Clutter writes to Mr. Clear. It is a portrait of the interior of the brain, I believe.

My father died, before Christmas. Swiftstyle, on the hoof, driving in his car, he and Alice, on a stormy Sunday north to his bus people. He must have just seized up, totally. Alice said he turned off at a ramp, unaccountably, and just kept on going. Through everything. They were on I-91 in Windsor. So I drove out after the memorial service just to have a look, and to clean out the car. The State Police had impounded it and the trim — grillwork and lenses and things — were still lying in the woods and bushes when I found the site. Adding up to roadside rubble. It must have been terrorizing. To both of them. I don't know, of course, but one imagines a moment's consciousness after a seizure of that kind, as with electrical shock. Seized muscles, pain, speechlessness, an inability to function (my memory of car claustrophobia) — yet the body's machinery of perception continuing to read: seeing, hearing, reflex instinct . . . a kind of drowning, or dream-watching consciousness, something like that. As well as to the people in the car behind them, who stopped. Can you imagine? Getting off at the exit ramp but not exactly by the recommended route.

Locked: in gear, locked to the right, locked on the accelerator. The car ripped through double cable and steel posts of the fence into thicket — great woody shrubs and trees down a 40-foot bank into swamp, a bumper-car slalom of a roller-coaster drop — trees gashed up by both sides of the car, broken off, dragged; then up through the swamp — by momentum, by careen, obviously — smashed a wooden fence at the back edge of a lawn. Then — still sharply to the right — turned a semicircle in the lawn and crashed back through the fence into a bog of standing water, and stopped — the car heading up, back, as if sensing the road . . . like a stock car battered up under the grandstand, wild to get back onto the track. I thought of Post in the apple trees, in Jonesboro. And of how maybe we want to go off, on the way out. Haig and bombs. Type-A personalities. We. I wish he could have told about it, his details. How they find lobstermen who have died, alone, on board their boats: the boats are seen turning tight circles, riderless horses, in the bay.

Alice said he heaved a couple of times, big, as if for breath. Blood came from his mouth. They both had seatbelts on and "nobody got hurt." Alice figures he just kind of exploded inside. The State Trooper talked with him while they waited for the ambulance. Alice's door jammed and they had to get her out the other side. That's about all I know.

What I do not know is what he said to the trooper. But troopers were friends of his — associated, more or less, with Uncle Mel, his brother, the one who ran the prison farm in Massachusetts. If I had to guess the dialogue, the waiting . . . How's all the bad boys, hey Dinny? If he still had his wits about him. Then Mel himself must have been there, soon after, on the other side, to help him through — if anyone was. They say they do.

And so we have been to Connecticut. Three times, in fact — both before and after Christmas. And Christmas to Rochester. He left everything to Bob and me, and he was a collector (you thought my skill was self-taught?). How understandable, then, that he did not feel more at home among George's heaps on the island. One man's meat being another man's . . . erstwhile meat. I think that if we had each appointed the other, exchanged a summer week, to curate the other man's wealth, we both might have lived in clearer landscapes, cleaner rooms. I am thinking in fact how I might like to hire you now, some day when I'm off the island. Or a trade: I take your trees, you truck my trash. Big bonfire. The pagans used to do that every spring, ritually, to cleanse the spirit and encourage the sun.

But he was a giver, too. He was generous with things he felt there might be "some use" for, and he seemed to love most the situations within which he could both save and give. His tour-escort job got him a free pass on the Greyhound and he came Thanksgiving this year with the turkey in his suitcase thawing, on schedule. All with tape cassettes of music he had recorded and thought we might like, and disposable plastic razors, rubberbanded in a bunch like small carrots, which he'd picked up on sale somewhere (10 cents instead of 20) and knew I liked — remembering his words last May at George's, as to how I do look better keeping clean of face, "even out here" — on the farm — even if I "won't be seeing anybody." Backsliding, though, being understandable, considering. It's rough on parents. There is too much history, too much whatever — Stephen's shirts, for a fact, have not been right lately and I can't see his eyes for ragged bangs, and he won't wear boots in snow to the bus.

And so he gave his opinion, too. Saved this, gave that. Saved his money, gave his skin. Literally. You've heard it said about "saving one's skin?" He was carrying in his wallet when he died three cards, signed and witnessed, directing his disposal, piece by parcel. His skin to the Children's Burns Hospital, a Shriners' project in Boston, for skin grafts. He was a Shriner and sold tickets to the circus. He left his eyes and kidneys for surgical parts, transplants. In fact "any other useful organs" it said on the card — a kind of discretionary fund of spare parts. It sets you to wondering what you might run across in the garage. Image of John Carmon, the aspiring mortician at the cocktail party, on trade perquisites: " . . . your drunks, your derelicts, and your jumpers." Apparently it's been upgraded since and you can sign on. For quality, I should think — picturing the eyes of a jumper. Wild. The kidney of a derelict, the noses on your drunks. Dad was serious about this and liked the idea — had spoken about it more than once, as something personal but also, somehow, apart from himself. Larger, maybe. For healing. For life. (And for free — a Dinsmore to the end!) To feel that he was helping somebody in some way always pleased him, big, made his day. He was against being taken, though, as a cadaver to a medical school tank. Use me live and bury the rest. Not Selzer, but John Prine. Please don't bury me / Down in that cold cold ground / No I'd druther have 'em cut me up and pass me all around / Throw my brain / In a hurricane / And the blind can have my eyes / And the deaf can take both of my ears / If they don't mind the size. / Give my stomach to Milwaukee / If they run out of beer / Put my sox / In a cedar box / Just get 'em out of here. . . / Sell my heart to the junk-man / And give my love to Rose / . . . Send my mouth / Way down south / and kiss my ass goodbye.

Finnegan Dinnegan's wake. I woke up last week with those words in my head, dreaming, something dreamt, vanished, like a phrase out of a forgotten song, and got up and stoked the stove. We are selling the house. We have been through everything. Every. Thing . . . In Dinnegan's wake. 40 years. They moved into the house three weeks before I was born. Paid around $6,000. The Realtor is asking 87,500 — already had an offer of $75,000. The stockpiles in the attic, the cellar, and the garage have increased by a similar multiple. In volume, not value. A lot I hadn't seen for thirty years; some things never. Joan and I are beginning to recognize more clearly our calling, that certain special something chosen for us: we clean up other people's houses, and move in boxes. Interstate experience. My old Soap Box Derby car still hangs in the garage. But it may go into the hometown museum! Like Hank Aaron and Willie Mays. Fame is relative. Smiling pickles. Even the factory is defunct. They will want my helmet and shirt, too. My medal in three colors, silken striped red, white and blue. It was the furniture auctioneer's idea, a man gifted in stirring up impulse over useless items. Put my socks / In a cedar box / Just get 'em out of here.

What do you do with things? What Dinnegan didn't do again. Though he had wanted to. The fathers eat grapes, the children's teeth are set on edge. We found some bags of dry split peas in the furnace room. After we had been back in Friendship a while we cooked up a potful — sweet, nice, an all-day scent risen from the woodstove. We loved them. I said to myself, I'll mention how we liked them, and thanks. Meaning in the next letter to him. It's tricky how it gains and recedes, a tide, the reality. Dad is dead.

What to do with things. Eat the peas. Peas is easy. Alcohol, too. I've got a bottle of beer, from out of the vegetable cellar, from the brewery where my mother worked, in the North End of Hartford, during the Depression. The New England Brewery. I thought of you and Hulls. And have got Emmy's autoharp down from the attic. And probably one of Tom Sharp's paintings. You wouldn't want to repossess the harp, would you? For Siobhan. Siren of the

Deep Cove shoals. Siobhan and Charybdis.

I have a tintype of my Grandparents Dinsmore, young, from Truro, Nova Scotia — around 1885. Dad brought a copy at Thanksgiving he had had made. Auntie Blanche wants the tintype back, unfortunately, and so I lose my companion piece to George. She is the survivor now, of the eight of them. My grandmother, Jesse, as a girl, was shot in the forehead by a village idiot, so alleged, and was visited in her sickroom by Queen Victoria. The Queen was on tour of the Commonwealth and just happened to be in the neighborhood. I think some of the leaden matter got passed down, so to speak, through Gramms's heirs, genetically, finding its way into my pants. Tintype to leaden-type. Reverse alchemy. The degeneration gap. My eight years of report cards from Sunset Ridge School have been recovered from the attic. Mrs. Levine, in school longhand: "James is a superior student. Often he does not use his time to his best advantage." I am thinking of asking her to rough out my eulogy. Our lives are transparent. There is a lot will be forgotten. Father, mother — both gone now. It makes a body feel a little older — and left out. Or in. The game. 40 seems to be the year, or, one of them. The Coach clearing the bench. Get the lead out, hey . . . ! Back onto the field for the start of the third quarter, a faint familiar hollowness pitting into the gut. Dealt with maybe. Hopeful. An ulcerous optimism I don't think will be changing very much.

Here, that day of the accident, we bore up under cold sleet and a gale of wind. One of those colossal birch trees on George's Bank leaned out too far and collapsed onto the beach. Whether quietly or not we can't say. But with an overload of fat crows in the branches, likely, and ice. Our morning surprise. It was an action displaced, a monument — and set down in about as good a place as any. . . .

Meantime, our house is coming along. I think that it will always be "coming along." When not in the deep freeze, as now. When Dad died we were just into the closing December stage, ahead of the winter. Sudden tailspin then. Getting to Connecticut, getting back. Will it snow? How do you just up and leave for a week in December? And boats. And go back to it. A year ago the bottom dropped out, sub-zero, wind, ice, bitter — the first week of December. Well, we were lucky. Fine weather for the funeral. We got back and simply took up where we had left off. We were still spared of snow, even though it was quite cold for working out there, very little sun. Joan learned how to wear eight quilted layers on her uppers, five on the lowers. I couldn't tell her from the cat on cloudy days, except that she was bigger and seemed to walk upright. We had a week to finish everything, until April. We were scheduled on Saturday to meet back in East Hartford and start in on the attic. Then Joan fell off George's kitchen roof.

I am not making this up. She landed flat on her back. Flat. From eight feet, from over the door, onto a sheet of plywood on frozen ground, in the total dark. Simply stepped backwards off the edge, like a frogman over the gunwale into water. This was Thursday, at night.

We were working to finish the kitchen roof — the upper rafters, insulation, pink paper, rails, decking. Snow was predicted for Friday, a mess. And then Connecticut. So we worked all day Thursday, very well, the end in sight. We were fitting the plywood when it got dark. It was cold. But we were delighted with the job, an end, optimistic, deciding to finish by flashlight rather than in snowfall in the morning. It was then mostly a matter of driving nails (gloved hands) and then boarding everything up for the storm.

We were right at the end of the job. The sky pitch black by now, steam of breath in the beam of flashlight — hammering the last nail. Literally. Joan stood over me, holding the light. Then sudden darkness. I could not see to hammer. And turned, to wonder why — rather out loud — she could not hold the forking flashlight fixed on one more forking nail before she quit . . . ? But Joan was not there. She had vanished. And then, out over the edge I saw the flashlight on the ground. I don't know whether she was holding it. Pained, breathless whimper. A keening. A sound not human. Distant, almost — of the night.

We were two hours getting off the island. For an hour and a half Joan lay on the ground or just crawled, first here, then there — cold crust of George's lawn — fearful of trying to get up, for her back. Trying to keep a quilt on her, things under her, talking to her, the tide going, and the dory high up on the beach ground-

ing out. She was talking urgently, incessantly, a babble which seemed at once coherent and insane, as out of sleep. You say I fell off the kitchen roof? You fell off the kitchen roof. Do you know where you are? We're at George's but I don't know why. I can't remember coming. You say I fell off the kitchen roof? Disbelief, bewilderment. What was I doing on the kitchen roof? We were building the roof. Can you get up? Do you think you're going to pass out? I think I hurt my back. I think it's okay, I think my back is okay. You say I fell off the kitchen roof? At George's? I have no idea what I'm doing here, I can't remember coming. We came this morning, in the dory. Do you remember that? We've been working here all day. No, I can't. You say I fell off the kitchen roof? Do you have a headache? No. I hurt my back, don't move me! I think my back is all right. I have no idea what we're doing here. You say I fell off the kitchen roof? The kitchen roof? Why was I up on the kitchen roof? We were boarding up the roof. You can't remember doing that? Joan? You were holding the flashlight for me. It's going to snow tomorrow and we wanted to finish. Can you remember going out to get the dory before it got dark? Hesitation. Crying . . . a grimace arrested, as in pain. It's dark?

Bewilderment. Oh . . . I'm sorry, Jim . . . to do this. To be scaring you like this. You must be scared. I think I'm all right. I don't know why I'm here. I fell off the roof? You say I fell off the kitchen roof? Yes. We have to get in the dory. The tide's going. Can you get up? I think so. Don't move me, I think I hurt my back. We have to get in the dory? Where's the dory? You say I fell off the kitchen roof? Yes. We have to go home. The dory is on the beach. You went out and got it before dark. Crying . . . I don't remember. Don't let me get cold. Keep me warm. Joan, tell me if you think you're going to faint. I don't think I'm going to faint. Can you crawl to the bank? We have to get in the dory. You say I fell off the roof? Yes. We have to go home. To the mainland. Do you remember where we're staying? Silence, crawling, a faint whimper . . . No. We're staying at the Spears'. We are? At the Spears'? Crying. Yes. Joan, it's all right. Sarah and Stephen are there now, but probably wondering where we are. Yes — our children . . . Oh Jim . . . I'm so sorry to be doing this to you . . . I'm all right, really I am. I'm getting a little cold. Wrap me up. I don't

should advise him about the door popping open. He sat perched and bounced easily with the roots, a smooth-faced, alert, contented man — his profile against the crazed pattern of cracks in the door window glass which, together with the other broken windows, betrayed to the symbol of his figure a violent, barbarous aspect to the nature of life on the island — of ours, of Ross, who was coming home, a secret glimpsed. I was two days unshaven, thought of the gift of dime razors, my father's wise counsel. We hadn't known of this, an accident of meeting that morning in the harbor, with Ronnie: . . . be bringing Ross out today on the high water, how's that truck of yours workin'?

Small talk with the minister, pleasing, as between strange partners on horseback, one a guest. I thought of my days in the faith, traveling to exotic churches, outposts — bands of dusty Chinese guiding British clerics with trunk and baggage through Asia, nineteenth century, the assurance of God in the world, and healing. The truck's gas pedal had unhinged beneath my foot and vanished through the hole in the rotting floor — a sort of shedding, or willful amputation, in accord with some built-in sense of technological equilibrium: the obvious and just answer to no brakes is no gas pedal. The Lord will provide. The part will be collected from the field one day by the curious and examined among the disgorged pellets of owls. I had made the thing myself when the truck was new to us from Johnny Neubig and the floor less rotten, and I have had to revert to the old method he taught me involving a toe to wobbly throttle knob — kind of like picking a marble out of a cup with your toes in a wool stocking. The minister showed interest in the island and was surprised at how "far" we had to go for the burial. An illusion of vehicle jostle, I think, and wincingly close scenery branches snapping at the door, mule-lurch, engine noise — that is the genius of those tiny, marvelous rides to forever at Walt Disney World. He asked where we lived. The layout we viewed in a moment from out of the woods put the processional car in the Mercedes class. You expected the heads of trolls to pop up by the bridge, or of Michael and Jesse in the red cart, sporting with them, to pay their respects to the passing dead. It was Disney's version of Yawknapatawpha County, the Pope on tour with Fellini's clowns going up with Faulkner to Jefferson. I

wanted to ask for ritual blessing, the province of some saint whose grace could see us through. . . . I don't believe I'll ever see it. . . . But wasn't that the blessing? His approval; Ross's province. I might come live with ya.

The grave was clean-cornered and professional, prepared early in the day at a site technically outside the cemetery (which is said to be "full") — on Raymond's land, just below the grave of Raymond's brother Kenneth, the one they called "Bear," whom we remember being buried when the frost went out, in March, that first winter we lived on the island. There was a kind of which-end-is-up discussion over Ross, settled concisely, on semantics. Hall the mortician: Facing east means the head toward the west. Ronnie: When we say the wind is to the east'rd, it's comin' from the east. Ross's alignment with the stars. It focused things. It set the rite as a primal reiteration I had forgotten was important to us still — the rising and setting of the planets, phases of the moon, navigation at sea, astrology, the tides, plantings, light and gravitation, the diurnal cycles that Ross by his camp window had been so attuned to in his living. Positioning in nature, the way a cat finds its spot by familiarity, by lightfall, by whatever else — centrality, or balance. We lowered him with ropes, blue coffin into a fresh pine box. Then the minister spoke. The Bible open. Passages. We all stood ragged-file at the edge of the hole and listened, a pickup crew, captive, able — a one-night stand in church. It seemed right. Blackflies around the face in the silence. Funerary scripture. I don't know whether it was many rooms in my Father's mansion but it should have been — Ross had one of them — three windows, a stove, and a 6 ft. ceiling. The Lord's Prayer in a head-bowed choral mumble. Bernard stood beside me. Speechless gaze, eyes focused inward. The gravediggers, lacking a hammer, pounded nails into the lid with stones from the earth pile. It was primitive. You wanted to offer them a thigh bone. But it was good for that, too. Simple, basic, respectful — true. Joan went back later on and set in by Ross a tiny patch of johnny jumpups. Ross had taught us to call them pretty-faces, the name he'd learned. They had spread over the winter in the garden, just above the pea rows by the fence. All bright and blooming tiny in the sun before we even got to the garden this spring, the year's first blossom.

Raymond died. Found aboard his boat Tuesday on the mooring. He had rowed out from Evelyn's, was to have his boat hauled out on the high water for the winter. Huge crowd for the services in Waldoboro, people standing. Then many to the island on Buddy's boat for the burial, next to Ross. SW blowing fog, warm, thick. Ghost ship, late afternoon Nov. light. Tide at half mast, going. They carried him up from the beach. West wall of his grave Ross's pine box, unaged. The graveyard grown tall since May, dry November browns, seeds, ruptured pods. Bed of mem. flowers now, Raymond's, bright still, that frost at night: 2 floral anchors, a white heart (Florence), a helm, a wreath, and a potbuoy of chrysanthemums in his colors ("Friend") — looking awfully like a jug. Green and orange. Green and yellow / Mother-be-quick-and-lay-me-down-to-die. Sad, sad here.

FALL 1982

We received and have posted, Jed, your poster, rumpled from its wrap, somewhat after the manner of the Hostess Twinkie of Boy's back pocket, years ago. The mailman may have figured the illusion of, or aging crush, to be to advantage as investment while we stay the course of Depression. I thought of Stark's friends this week (the ones whom my old truck, for lack of brakes, sent leaping last summer into Josephine's alders and blackberry thorns) when Sotheby's sold for half a million dollars Stravinsky's manuscript of a young girl dancing herself to death, wildly, ritually, in his head. Art is worth the price collectors pay, and we are glad in your poster to have yet the dory we once had and yet to have rid of it — and gain the cash. She being nicer on the wall, in portrait, than sat in on the chop. I had thought the show to end in Oct. It happens that we had planned anyway to perambulate through Boston over Thanksgiving and so will detour by Andover. The title is comic, if not threatening, for rarefaction — Latin cognitive — and I worry that Harold will be taxed for his thing by Augusta. We wonder how your photograph qualified, unless

Harold be found to have a perambulator tucked away in there somewhere. You should photograph Dan Winchenbaugh's shop and see what they interpolate. Surely would Harold more love a ride in one now, being somewhat lighter of limb lately than on that day of his restless, ghosted sitting for his portrait (PL. 10).

Which hangs well here: Harold's shop open to the rafters — an interior, dim extension of Art's bright room — like some old, dark wing of this building, where the dory looms — white. It is Moby Dick hung by strings from the ceiling of the Peabody. Blubber and bone-chip on the floor. Harold sits with the mutilated patience of a whaleman — Ahab, doing scrimshaw.

Thinking of Harold, I think of pickle scent of wood shavings in that shop, of urine in sawdust, abstracted to the air by stove heat — the pickle scent of my Grandfather Bliss living with us, not quite 88, who died on my birthday when I bought the Davy Crockett record. I think of Ross and Harold, old men in their eighties, the legend of hard, frontier boozing together, their own sordid tales, long quit now — Ross relating to us the kind of outrage he felt about Harold's being, as he said, "got into it" — rum-hard, driven, by older, taunting men in the boat shop, by a kind of cruelty, a tainted humor fashionable to that day which I associate with sweatshops and the Industrial Revolution, or with episodes of Huck Finn on the river — involving fools, crude wit, outwit — power by exploitation of the unwitting, the tender, and the gullible. And I think, beyond these, to diabetes — of loss, of going to pieces — in pieces — piecemeal — bladder, diet, the leg amputation: of Boynton; his life, dead thirty years his junior. Of work in Maine. Harold and Peter: dories and stories.

Dories as stories — rambulations — hunky, burly. Boys and men / 3 score and ten / lost from Grimsby town. . . Swift, neat-worthy. And of Harold's boy — "He would have been about

----

I met Harold Benner only once. I photographed him in his workshop alongside the road to Waldoboro. He was building a dory for Jim. That picture was used on a poster the Addison Gallery of American Art made for an exhibition called "New England Perambulations." Jim refers ironically to this title because by the time of the exhibit, Harold had lost a leg to diabetes.

your age "... Harold got him off the island, sick, in the middle of the night, to Damariscotta. Who suddenly then, a while after, just died — sent away, to home, the boy and his Dad, by the Doctor's missed diagnosis. "You never get over it, 'twas many years ago..." New England perambulation, stark, Puritan death. "You've kids of your own," Harold said, "I know y'do. Wife a pretty woman."

I'm going to jury duty. The clerk of Knox County has summoned me to sit for 15 days in judgment of my peers, in the Superior Court next month in Rockland. It seems like a calling, one of those accidents of elevating titillation — Why me? — on the road to Damascus, and I seem to have no choice but to go. A new niche in my career. I'll have to dress again. My first day in school. I arrive headstrong with innocence, with a child's naivete about Right and Order, and with a compulsive curiosity — prurience, even — about the issues that are fought over in the world of grownups. For credentials, I come presenting total darkness, the portfolio of the blank page — am plucked fresh off the farm with dung on my boots, green — the way they want me. Experience, though, is it, of the flashy, hi-shooting sort — what folks in the kitchens uptown work out mentally, codelike, on the red nervous knobs of their police-call scanners, printing out verdicts. Like video game — that grand garble behind the locked doors of the brain — privy of judges — the shadowy, soulless monologue of whispers from down under... and it seems unfair to be asked to make it all official now, out loud and in the papers. Do they ask a Sunday beer-drinker to call the huddle? Suit up and get grass stains on his shirt? End-around or the option: Statue of Liberty. Here I stand. Dinny meets the Bad Boys.

I shrink, and can feel already the curl of my knuckles tightening around the stone I fumble from my pocket. James Joyce

Peter Boynton was a professor of Jim's at Wesleyan and a life-long mentor. He owned a small island off Stonington. Boynton began writing novels relatively late in his life, and the two books of his that I have read, Games in the Darkening Air *and* Stone Island, *are lyrical, brooding accounts of life in Maine. Boynton died suddenly one summer while in Hawaii — a loss that Jim never got over.*

sights the city dogs. The stone I would send hurling on signal at that poor bastard waiting in the dock....

But there is a difference between spring training and the Game, and likely I am as ready as I'll ever be to step out of my Winterhaven and the sun into the gray, chilly league of Hard Knox. Ivan on the beach with a rubber hose. What are the stories? The wardens seized 24 men last night on a freighter in Bremen, Round Pond (a stone's throw, so to speak, from here) with 30 tons of bales in her bilges — which didn't look much like traps stocked astern and it wasn't baled buckwheat for the barn. Swash-buckling sea dogs from Rockland, Tenants Harbor, Waldoboro, Bremen... and Ann Arbor, Michigan. How much of a batch would a Winchen batch if a winchen would batch bales? (Two.) Including the Colombian crew, the vessel, rediscovering America for the Spanish queen — in the eight-o'clock dark of new moon at the lobster wharf, who slur the lobstermen's tongue, their shibboleth. Dialogue: E'yuh. Just down f' the weekend?... And one "former Chairman of the Maine Liquor Commission," caught corrupting his alcohol with weed roughage, the new fruit salad. A bust of busts. The Commissioner's daughter ran for reelection to the State Legislature. Her own bust was less memorable, though also given to public scrutiny in the papers and a vote. It all came out in the wash. The Maine Yankee referendum did badly as well. The referendum quite possibly came down to an anti-drug vote in the end — pro-America. T-shirt: Nukes yes. Pukes no.

There is a certain contraband-mentality in the countryside — probably dating from the days when all known territory was claimed for either Jerusalem or George II — whereby trouble is perceived as arising not from within but by arrival — by shore-landing, invasion, encroachment — from "out of state," or "from away." One would think that for that reason alone they would throw the Nukes out. But something about it, the glitter and hum of high-tech living, the new Hardware Store down river seems to have an irresistible appeal — stainless, clean — magical. In business. Frugal Yankee trade, independent, self-regenerating. We gather round the Sony on the cracker barrel to watch our heroes land: the Columbia shuttle ship, the Colombian shuffle. Silver and gold. The spaced voyagers. The erstwhile, old-time smugglers here, of Prohibition days, occupy a nostalgic corner of sea-going folklore. Rum runners are remembered, it seems as somehow more solid in their trade, a home-grown native shrewdness to their corruption. Boys will be boys. A cleaner act — Prometheans reclaiming their belly-fire from the Law — heroic, justifiable partly for the fact that rum and fish have been historically inseparable on the Georges Bank — since at least the days of the earliest British fishing camps set up along the savage coast. But today it is a dirty business. Foreign, swarthy, scruffy, a cancerous and dispiriting threat to the basic fabric. One crew intercepted off Stonington last year are to claim in court next month that it is the stuff of "our religion" — intended not for sale but for sacrament, for church — the wine and wafer. 34 tons. Church and State, it's their Constitutional exercise. All in all, thorny philosophic cases that will be going to the Feds, fortunately, in Portland.

Still, the papers promise enough sordid wreckage to go around. Or, in the event of slow going, the Clerk advises me to show up with a good book or my knitting. Nothing much new — I've been hoping to show up with a book for quite a while; but as to knitting in court. . . the heart falters under the cool, immortal needles of Mme. Defarge and the justice guillotine. The only bright spot is the pay. The governor has pledged $20 / day each day I show up for work plus 15 cents / mile for the drive round trip to the Court House. I get to start Dec. 6th.

Which happens to be the anniversary of my father's death.

Which makes a sobering body nervous to wonder about the scale of this sort of work and at which Judgment we be asked to sit. Still, 15 cents a mile round trip to the right hand of the Father adds up, surely, to a bundle. Shoot the moon. Space walk — way, way out, the long shot. My ticket on the horses, Elijah's fiery chariot, the trip of astronauts 15 cents a mile in a million dollar suit. Worth the gamble, I feel, since nothing else I do makes a nickel. Ask my inlaws. I have found my work in pardons.

Prine: Father, forgive us for what we must do / You forgive us, we'll forgive you / We'll forgive each other / Till we both turn blue / Then we'll whistle and go fishin' in Heaven. . . .

We do get out, though. Church and the laundromat are gathering places, spirit lifters in the off season. Joan had a whole machine-load gathered up for her — all the blues — up and out, gone, from the laundromat in Waldoboro. A couple hundred dollars at least, replacement. It tends to crack the door to paranoia. In town the eye roams to size up bodies — India blouse, jeans, corduroys — an attention to neighbors' tastes toward the blue end of the spectrum. Bad, depressing. Not having the blues is worse than having them.

Ken Cady got into some wash of his own. He and Mary were in Boston calling on Edith, Mary's mother, in the hospital. While waiting for the elevator, Ken slipped somehow and went down — whole kit and kaboodle — onto the fresh-mopped wet floor and lay writhing, speechless, clutching his knee. He soon after found himself laid out in a white bed of his own on the same floor with Edith. In agony. His kneecap had all smashed to pieces — bad, very. They had him in traction, or whatever, and I don't know what all — it was months ago and I can't remember. He still suffers. A gruesome story, a terror. Death by banana peel. It's bad enough just being there at all — for a visit — let alone rolling around on the floor in all that wet, hospital mop pickle. It seems like some sniper scheme for the hospital industry. I couldn't help thinking of Michael's story about Ken's misadventure with the supper-table bench, one summer years ago, while dining with the Pratts on the island. Drinks were down, and then some, and guests going for their seats at table. Ken was to share a bench. Somehow in the shuffle Ken got himself perched out of balance on the thing and started tipping backwards, arrested for a moment in the air, in a kind of near-equilibrium (you have to make Michael tell it, for the Borst range of audio-visuals). Ken's arms flew up behind, scooping tread-water circles in the candle-lit air, grasping to regain balance by gyration, uttering little cries as the arms spun — Wu, wu-wu — rhythmic owl-like sounds — Wu! wu . . . ! — incantatory, as if the call could woo him back — Wu! Wu! Woo! Woo! — to equilibrium; but it was too late. Over he went, backwards, in a great suppertime crash and a heap, while the dinner party looked on, aghast and helpless. No one could have prevented it. Before anyone understood what was happening it was over. Balance, to the Oriental mind, is a delicate business. It is achieved as by instinct, effortlessly, by non-action. To the Chinese it is in accord with the Doctrine of Wu-wei, or "non-action according to the Tao." It may be that Wu-wu is about as close as we in the West can come to the inscrutables. In any case, no one much acted in this instance, and Ken, Michael says, retreated to the bathroom to regain his senses. The Tao knows the power of the quiet pool. Poor Ken. Life is all just dress rehearsal of one good act, with variations. . . .

I caught the fishhouse squirrel. Varmint of the nibbly destruction. In October, when we were doing the steel. Each morning, for days, my apple would be stolen from the rat trap. It was increasingly incredible for the hair-trigger set to the thing, a game. Then one morning while moving planks I happened just by chance to corner it, not six feet away. We faced off in shared confusion — sudden barn-hollow silence. Split the plank and there is Jesus. Neither of us risked a move. There was the strange, energizing sensation of total focus, catlike, in a hunt — solitary, absurd, everything abandoned but the weight of the moment, the confrontation. Wrestlers' foreplay before the tangle on the mat. Then the squirrel jumped and I trapped it with the flat side of a hoe. There was a lot of squealing, wiry-muscled struggle in soft fur. My other fell to bludgeoning the animal with a stick of firewood. Jimmy Carter once clubbed a swimming rabbit that had sidled up to the Presidential canoe. I am a peace-loving man. The talk of geese in the radar scope launching the warheads takes on new meaning. I am glad not to have command of the button.

Meanwhile, on another shore of the island, a squirrel seems to be making cushy quarters in the fiberglass roof insulation, where we left it open at the ridge pole. The cat has asked that I leave the family till spring. The weekend after Raymond died, in November, I was busy forking seaweed onto the potato patch, enjoying the low sun — a gift in that month — when blasts of six shotgun volleys issued from the woods at my back. It seemed like point blank. Argentine commandos in the Falklands. I think my hat inflated with the compression. I yelled: "Hey . . . !" and there was a sudden, wild crashing of sticks and brush and in the next moment a deer charged galloping out of the woods, a heavy buck — rack of antlers — and turned when it saw me, maybe ten yards away, and galloped off down the wood road. It sounded like a

horse, the hoof-pound on hollow ground, the soundtrack of a western, an earth-sound strangely out of place out there to me, wallowing in the potato furrow, the beach manure. Then — galloping out of the woods — Albert appeared. Rifle and orange knit hat, the stubby red beard — "You see that deer, Jim?" — quick of breath, quicker of foot, a way I had never seen him. I pointed, and he stood for a second, then dashed back into the woods in the direction he'd come from, toward Arthur's house. "I shot at two. One's still in he'ah." If I had seen only one, then the other had run a few yards then fallen, or else was hiding, lain down. It seemed in that moment like an invitation — a search mobilization — and I drew into the woods, found myself following, suddenly vulnerable for the feel, when once in the woods, of no bright clothing on my body. I skipped up my pace and drew up behind Albert, suddenly boys together and he was my big brother. We were down Arthur's slope, where he had shot at the deer, and I stood at the edge of the field, as if positioned, posted, while Albert went into the brush — sumac and juniper and alders — then the spruce woods beyond, Raymond's land, with the white birches. I could hear him tramping around in there, for what seemed like a long time — maybe five minutes — and he had not driven the deer out in my direction, and so I followed in behind him. We were within seeing distance of each other and we seemed perplexed and convinced that the deer was lying in there somewhere, right around us — wounded, or dead, or just hiding. I have watched the cat lose a caught mouse in a thatch of tall grass and scratch around where she last saw it, and pounce and probe, and paw, and pace up and down, and just sit. We scratched around for a while, the two of us, less urgent now for the time lapse, and circled finally back up the slope and came out on the path, and it wasn't until then that I saw Ronnie, down towards the other end of the path, walking up from the graveyard. Sudden presence. The cemetery. They had laid Raymond in there on Thursday. This was Saturday. Ronnie and Albert had been pallbearers when our old truck had refused to work for a dead battery. The heaped bed of flowers and the flag on Raymond's grave were still as fresh this morning as summer daisies, despite the nighttime frost. Joan and I had stopped by, off the path, early, on the way in from the Graveyard Pt. offhaul. "One took off," Albert said, "down Jim's road. The others's layin' in here. There was two. I know I hit one."

They discussed things a minute, then Albert said he couldn't be absolutely sure; the other deer might, just might possibly, have escaped to the shore, towards the Gut, when he undertook to chase the big buck up from Arthur's. Ronnie was looking me over — black hair under his orange brimmed hat, the broad face, trim moustache of a woodsman — tall — with the same kind of handsome in his face that Ross had, his uncle, but on that big youthful body of his. He seemed to accept me as part of the hunting party, expected there, a recruit.

"You say that deer run right by you?" "I yelled when I heard the shots," I said, "Well then," Ronnie said, " — why didn't you get him with that pitchfo'ak?"

My hand still clutched the seaweed dungfork — taken to it like Yaz to a Louisville Slugger, dragging it around the park — a Minuteman drafted out of the field, without time enough even to alert his woman in the kitchen. Dry, purple clots of seawrack clung to the base of the tines, like strands of hog's gut. Ronnie with a rifle, Albert with the shotgun . . . and Jim joining up with his dungfork, who let the beast get away — the only clean shot of the expedition. Neptune would have used one on a fish. And Satan might have had a dungfo'aked tail. I've never been very professional about my rigging. " . . . I didn't know who you were," I heard myself telling Albert. I was feeling disruptive, unhunterly, about the Hey! "I didn't know who . . . might not know we were here."

Ronnie looked at me — blue, tolerant eyes. Cheerful, confident still somehow, it seemed, of the hunt. "We know where y' are," he said. Albert was starting back into Raymond's woods. Orange stubble of cheekbone and chin below the bright orange wool hat. Fire chief. "We won't shoot 'cha, Jim," Albert said. "We ain't that kind."

Next day on the wharf Ronnie told me they had followed tracks and spotty blood "halfway the length of the island." Then had come off the island at dark with nothing, neither of the deer. They figured the other one might have swum across the Gut. It was most of a week before we heard shots again. Five big blasts — spaced apart this time, from the direction of Ivan's shop. It was late afternoon, low tide, dead flat calm. We had been boarding up the north wall, lost in the hollow solitude of our own hammering. The blasts echoed like cannon from a frigate in the bay. Later on, after dark, the carcass hung gutted from the boom on Buddy's fish wharf. They were rinsing it out with the bait hose when we got to the harbor. Antlers. The big buck. Albert had the liver and heart in a plastic bag, looking like dark fish flesh. The heart was for sandwiches, he said. Ronnie told how he had posted himself on the roof of Josephine's tool shed near the outhouse, expecting the deer to come out of the woods before dusk to feed in Jose's orchard. It did though from the direction of George's, behind Ivan's camp. The direction was unexpected, because of our hammering, and Ronnie turned to position himself and wait for the buck to enter the apple trees. But in turning, an edge of Ronnie's boot caught a roof shingle, he said, and made a little scuff — Ronnie dragging his leather boot to show — a tiny sound; and when he did, the buck seized up and looked right at him. Ronnie knew he had to shoot. The deer was still well off — out of decent range — way down at the field's edge by Delbert's old rotting Studebaker. It stood staring straight at him, waiting for Ronnie to make another move. The aim would be for the head so as not to waste meat. He fired and hit the buck in the shoulder (Ronnie showing us the big hole — crimson-black — in the left shoulder of the hanging carcass). The buck turned and began running toward the shore. Ronnie fired again. The buck kept running, he said. Albert, all this while, was down behind the bank somewhere, near the edge of the woods, and when the deer, running towards him, caught sight of the second hunter he suddenly lay down in the bushes to hide. Ronnie by now was down off the roof and running a little sou'west of where the buck had gone down, hoping to drive him east towards the shore and keep him out of the woods. Indeed, when the buck jumped, Ronnie shot again and the deer headed off for the shore — down over the bank onto the beach, between Ivan's shop and the brook, where Albert, who had been laying for him there, shot him dead. I think he said he shot him in the head. It was the deer that had galloped past me down onto the wood road almost a week before.

Next morning, early, my approach in the dory flushed a gang of crows from the stone beach by the mouth of the brook. The tide had left a clot of gutted innards. They lay like jellyfish among the rocks and clay and yellow beachgrass, glossy and fresh in the November early sun. More than this once have I wished to have learned anatomy, dissections, instead of chemistry. A body entered is, to me, mush and tube and bubble. My own soft engine room laid out for inspection. Pinks and pale whites, thread veins, purple paste. I used to marvel that my classmates, in another lab, could cut open a frog and find anything, sort it all out. In post mortems they arrange you piecemeal in a succession of plastic trays, take slices and read your past on the slides of a microscope. The sum total, Judgment Day of the flesh, when the soul has fled to another court. Whereas the ancients divined in broken innards not the past but the future. A step into the sacred territory — taboo — a probing visit to the underworld, under flesh, down under, where secrets are hid, one's destiny arranged. The crows had plucked a hole into the deer's bloated stomach — a wine bladder on the beach with the bung popped. They had obviously favored the deer's diet, belly to belly, direct, the bilious green fiber mush, a veritable hairball of dense flossy tangle, a squirrel's nest of roughage packed away. Lacking a crow's bill, I probed a little with a stick. A mix from pate (Jose's apples?) to ripped unchewed leaves, grass blades intact, as if transplanted to take root. I got to thinking about food groups and balance, the darks and the brights, the buck's yin balancing with his yang, his valleys with his mountains. I wasn't able to locate his yang. Audubon might recommend we adjust the agenda in our garden and leave the gate open at nights. The only secret divined out of the belly of the beast was the whereabouts of our turnip tops. Which actually had been no secret at all, since he'd left his footprint behind. Still, it was nice seeing our vegetables again. Keep eating your beet greens and parsley, I'd say. I can only hope my own stomach will look half as healthy when some receding tide leaves it on the stone for inspection. Picture picking through the interior paste of the Hostess Twinkie girl.

The garden had a record feed this fall: 6 1/2 truck loads of seaweed, heaping, heavy — the springs flattened right out straight.

five from your beach, the rest from Jose's. Clean, pure, much of it compressed, rotting already — minimum of plastic trash, beercans and such. We had perfect storms — direction and tide. Your beach had a three-foot bank of it, a sheer ridge up to the thigh. Unprecedented. Then we sowed winter rye. If crops fail next summer, we'll eat the fertilizer. The Japanese call it "sea vegetables."

We've been enjoying your trees in our stove here, as before — your summer splitting. Thanks again! The getting of them to here, however, we did not enjoy, much. The warm late weeks of autumn refused to freeze your lower-level landscape: the bad luck of nice weather. The truck sank for the ledge like a stone through water — especially in the hollows of loose landfill. You won't need to plow for a garden. Nor irrigate. With a Disney audience and Jack Lemmon at the wheel the overloaded lurch and plummet might have been hilarious — escape through cannibal country with a load of poached ivory. Joan's laugh in the lonely forest was not convincing. The only thing achieving any escape was the tide. You can sketch in the rest. You've paid into that movie before, more or less. One pauses at such times to sort out the world's troubles. An honest day's work has no honor unto itself. No one ever labored harder than Sisyphus. Today he'd be shouldering his weight forward in a bread line, only to be ordered to the rear the moment his fingers unfolded to receive the loaf. God punishes us for the old virtues and for the simplest of ambitions.

But hear this, tell Jesse: big baseball is coming to Maine! (PL. 37) Have you heard? A Triple-A team connected with Cleveland, unnamed as yet ("Maine Indians" has been whispered) is moving to Old Orchard Beach — the Nantasket of Maine summers. Two hours from Friendship. They plan a stadium of 10,000 seats, ready for play in '84. The old "Charleston West Virginia Charlies." Driscoll on the mound and Beebs in the dugout. Book early! Beach sand, surf, hot dogs and the roller coaster. Passage on the ALDA E . . . if they can find someone to stand in for me. . . .

It's startling how far through we are to spring. It still thrills me, in some primal way, I suppose, to watch the sun's gain northward, mornings on the eastern horizon. Daily, steady. That you can see that, mark it — as kids mark the monthly gain in stature on the doorpost. The sunrise, from here, steps across Garrison Island now toward Bradford Pt. as by time-accelerated photography. If, to our hut-dwelling ancestors, there was any direct assurance of cosmic "renewal," it had to have been that. Even the bomb won't change that. That and the roaches. I remember Watts talking about how the bomb may simply be Earth's way of renewing itself into a star. The end-product of this planet's self-awareness, the experiment with human intelligence, a dazzling success. There seems a certain gathering volume of Apocalyptic allusion in the wind lately, along the lines of "Come, sweet Death." Robert Lifton's "psychic numbing" evolving into a psychic cuteness, spiritual euphoria, the "trip" to end all. Do you think they know what they are saying? Do we believe our own twaddle?

Maybe our luck will hold: in December, for just about a week, in glimpses, the island had another pink house! Ours. We insulated all the standing walls, raw side out, then boarded up fast and laid on the black paper. Bright pink wooly panels in that December sunny glare. Pink and black, 50's style, it was beautiful. The very day after, the sky all just went to pieces — wet and wild. But the water beaded up and rolled right off that black duck's back, tight and trim, way it should — a new sensation for us, I don't have to tell you. We went out next day in the storm's wake and just stood and looked at it a while, and it made us feel all kind of tucked in bed for the winter just to see it. Wanting to leave milk and cookies on the hearth. If we had a hearth. Life's great joys are simple, and probably regressive.

Well, this did get out of hand — this saga, this documentary novella — and I am sorry, believe me, to do this to you. Sorry even if just for the burden of its bulk — for just dropping it all on your doorstep, rolled up and let fly like the morning *Courant* I used to peddle. There is loss in the lapses. I won't even try to guess at the datings. But, it is a letter and it is to you. Obviously. Your presence wonderfully here in the writing of it — a self-granted honor and a luxury for me. I realize I did the same sort of thing to you about a year ago. I write and there are interruptions and I save it. I'll learn to send, to end arbitrarily. Things crowd in, urgently, more demanding, e.g., the insurance company. A pile of annoying correspondence and chasing for statements, which, fortunately, has just this week ended with most of a thousand dollars

additional money on the Rabbit's ocean voyage of last winter, off the wharf. (What we needed was spuds!) Boston mechanic found clamshells in the fan motor. The wheeze goes on. Our Rabbit is a varying hare. Front end, under the hood, promises itself one day the powdery, corrosive patina of bronze war statues and the flaking orange of old battleships. We're oxidizing here. Green and orange; Raymond's colors on the potbuoy. Green of his spruces and broad lawn, and of the sea; carrot-orange of his Florence's hair. Things fall apart. His boat came down through these waters this morning, by the western side of the island, a passage I never knew Raymond to take. The quiet and subtle changes. I don't listen, but I doubt the C.B. air gap has been filled, even now. Robins are suddenly this week everywhere around the bushes — the rose and the woodbine, the young apple trees, the gray hedge fence — driven, apparently, by these two enormous snowstorms of late. Audubon says that 80% normally will not survive the winter. If their preferred diet is the worm, they have lately converted to the freeze-dried berry and brown seed-husk. They scavenge like chickadees, an odd sight. Could it be that the sleeping worm of February lies curled within and they know it? Berried. These robins arrive, annunciating the spring, in three feet of snow, in February, rather in the way that Reagan reads his oracle promising the long-awaited boom. The groundhog yawns in the sunshine, retreats, reassuring his kingdom that winter has bottomed out; that we are already in the upturn, slow growth to summer. Fat Tuesday, licentious before the fast, purgatorial, to resurrection. For my part, the picture reads reliably below my east loft window. With the exception of a few battered old warriors, diehard regulars, the parade has passed by. Traffic on the Davis Point loop is down. An eerie quiet for here, even for winter.

Circulation is weak; the young swains have lost their motor reflex. Could be there's another Spanish freighter on the horizon, distracting the carnival to other streets. Whatever, the stillness is unnatural, the calm uneasy. We might do well to divert the Rabbit reimbursement money to cheap whiskey stocks and barrel-bottom wine. Carlo Rossi Red Paisano and, Boy's choice, Governor's Club Gold. Tony says we're going to be in this thing for a good long time.

Things are the same everywhere. We're buttoned up tight here, and keeping warm, and acquiring a good taste for the radon gas. It's elevating. Delirium radons. You wondered why those balloonists picked Maine as their starting point across the ocean. Joan blames it on "allergy" and walks around the house with a finger on her pulse. It's the new method, a form of masturbation, I think, when the batteries run down. There are books on it. I'm sticking with the alcohol, though, and calling it euphoria. Boy still calls it honk. Still floating when the tide goes out, an old seaman's trick.

"Practically finished" as a permanent state, a life style, has its advantages. You get to guest at places rather than host. When friends watch you work on the house they go away feeling accomplished, good about themselves. You enjoy thus the rewards had by therapists but without all the stress. Guest, calendar — as verbs. If host is verb then why not guest? "No, not me. I'm guesting this party." But calendar is a different matter. I'm verbing calendar, I think, because it says January 19, and I'm hoping it might move if I call it right. Like finding the right word to budge the cat. January 19, in England the Eve of St. Agnes, said to be the bitterest night of the winter. Below zero here, new moon. The wind northwest, bitter. It's no use verbing the cat, either. You should see her. The stove would sooner move than she. They huddle together as a kitten to its mother, in dusty dim lamplight. Four legs squat, and warm, sooty black. Mother roars to herself — remote, deep reverie, as a cat will — weighs 180 lbs. and eats wood all night. She is this village's version in cast iron of jungle idolatry, or the squatting, fat Buddha. Decorative breastplate gingerbread of mother cat teats. A provider. Opulent, indulgent. Fixed. Even the moon would not move tonight if she weren't still fleeing the sword of Orion. He is Pan chasing the nymph Syrinx, who escapes by growing fixed. It seems possible on nights like this that nothing may ever move again, that all things will stay forever put, or else shatter at the least touch. St. Agnes ascends into the nuclear age. It's reckless even to be trying to verb verb. . . .

Joe Cupo came on to do the weather tonight and said that the all-time coldest temperature ever recorded in Portland is 26 degrees below zero — the 19th of January, 1971. St. Agnes Eve. Spooky. Remember that winter? We arrived here before midnight, the sky black as molasses, and the whole cove was heavy ice — a surprise — a white desert. Next morning the surprise was sparkling blue water. The ice had broken while we slept and had moved out, vanished. We had not heard a sound. No storm, no thrash of wind. Somehow the fresh memory of it white, massive — the night deep and immense and still — made its disappearance ghostly, magical, an army encampment moving out soundlessly, without a trace. Drowsy visitation from Mars, gone by daylight. That weekend we found shrimp 3 lbs. / dollar at Harlan's and ate it seemed like buckets. We've improved our shelling method since.

Some nights, late, when conditions are right and Orion is just setting behind Bremen, the moon long gone, and long, long after the lobstermen have gone to bed (some may already be rising, a light switches on in a kitchen window), the star Bette (*Midler*) can be made out ascending the eastern sky. A constellation of one, a goddess, the divine Miss M. The ancients on shipboard implanted the star in her navel, a glittering diamond on black velvet. Fiery horses broken from Apollo's stable emblazon her hair, wild, driven, the slow, orbital gyration of her head as she ascends, the arc of her course through the heavens failing the fix of shipmen, Charybdis of the night sky (Bernard starts southeast'rd out of the harbor, ignores her, favoring the C.B.) the orbit of the diamond star the wavy swerve of the climbing red rose. To rosy fingered dawn, the first faint break over water. Venus, the morning star — blue now, paling — drifts from her stardom in the zodiac. Bernard picks up Portland. Do ya, dooya, dooya dooya dooya . . . Do you wanna dance?

I dreamt a while ago, a tiny, nervous dream, that the Spears were coming back, unexpectedly; and I woke and lay in bed all foggy and couldn't remember whether that meant we would be moving out or moving in.

It might be well to pack the potholder while we think of it. Worse. Unnerving: I worked late in Art's study the other night, got sleepy. In the morning a scrap of paper, typed, was stuck into the typewriter, a note to myself, so as to remind where to pick up.

It said: I keep waiting for word from south of here saying they have finally got someone to stand in for me.

I had no idea what it meant. I still don't. It related in no way that I could see to anything I was working on. Overnight, gone. With the ghost ice in the cove. It's like having film footage of a dream fragment totally forgotten, a frame-up. I do remember typing a note. When I get to jury duty everything's going to be simple and clear.

Eve of St. Agnes. Five thousand people in New York City shelters last night, the most since the Great Depression. Jesus Christ, are you there? To Reagan it's all just drainage. When the tide goes out, yachts all ground out together. Pass the duck l'orange.

I'll try to finish up the back issue right off and send it along. Most news will keep, even if dinner won't. Ross used to get his newspapers a month late by the crate and he lived to be 84. Whereas Ivan took his by daily dose and called it the Courier Guts-Ache. I'll see Bert again about your saw, pronto. Call collect if they find someone to stand in for me.

SPRING 1983

Days of grace now, sun pre-mosquitos, May's burst of tender shoots. Asparagus and fiddleheads, dandelions and daffodils, chives and spr. onions and the rhubarb. And peony's ruby bolt, like legs of a wading crane, inverted. Upside down with all this lovely busy.

JUNE 14, 1983

Stark came Mem. Day — looking rained on and blown about the Bay, and terrified. He called the chop "turbulent ebony." We met him in his yellow oilskins — including a laid-back sou'wester — taking a leak on Bill Hall's gravel in the rain. He had just come ashore to welcome a carload of weekend guests. The guests arrived and decided against the island for the holiday, and left. Whereupon Stark and his lady friend, and her flush-cheeked two-year-old, scrambled aboard the ALDA E. like refugees. We took their skiff in tow, and as we crossed the bay Stark told of his work in advertising now and of his parents' plans to visit England in early summer, and of his recuperation from recent hernia surgery ("It's in the family"). He had looked forward to some relaxation "and a swim" on the island over the long weekend. We set them adrift just past Bald Rock, boat people, the rain driving at their backs toward some foreign beach. Madonna and child bundled up in kapok. Stark's flight into Egypt, Gotham to Goshen. He's home again now and sent us a picture postcard of the Brooklyn Bridge.

We imagined you all celebrating the Centennial — was it the 24th? — with a bridge walk and sparklers. Then greeting Spider Dan on the Trade Tower. I pictured you in your window with binoculars following his progress, the day that I with mine chased a pair of scarlet tanagers from behind the garden up towards Arthur's, feeding in the blossoms of the wild pear. The last one I remember seeing sat perched one May in that monumental oak tree below the dooryard garden at Peter Boynton's house in Higganum, fifteen years ago. Peter said, "You won't find anything redder than that in nature." Unless it be Peter's own ruddy face — scarlet — cheeks and neck behind the frosty beard. I remember him sitting with the window open, late one afternoon after a sunny, brutal day in Stonington. Man mirroring nature.

Your apotheosis as a Japanese divinity will not, I hope, alter your style. The (shin) character, I think, actually looks like you — a stick figure drawing of you behind the tripod with your head stuck into the bellows. The last "former student" of yours

Stark Whiteley inherited the island's oldest standing house from the Wescotts. Paul Wescott painted seascapes from his studio overlooking Deep Cove. Stark recently curated an exhibition of many of those paintings for the Brandywine and Farnsworth museums. Stark's father, George, was a teacher and sailor who wrote Northern Seas, Hardy Sailors, *an account of life in Newfoundland. Stark drifts to his own drummer and his spacey exterior belies his brilliance and broad historical knowledge.*

casket, below Delbert's hands. He had fought in the War and, as the last rite of the service the head mortician and his driver gathered up the flag and, standing ceremoniously erect before the bereft, folded the flag the way we'd learned to years ago at dress parade in the Boy Scouts — with all of the snap and smartness of black-shoed Navy men. Then they presented it in its triangular form — white stars on a field of midnight blue — to Muriel. It was a patch of night sky, the stars gazed up at in February — hugely, incredibly — on a bitter moonless night from Delbert's granite doorstep on the island. Orion is rising to hunt the dark fields — a bounty on raccoon pelts. Taurus the bull at large again, snorting around, busted out to pasture from Lettie's barn. Cassiopeia's chair pulled up closer to the stove, the lamp, where Delbert's mother Lizzie sits to the light, darning. Comely Pleiades clustered — six of seven sisters (one hiding, shy, ashamed) — a dry stand of virgin wallflowers tittered at by pesky gusts of wind behind the "Old Maids' Paradise . . . ." Constellations commit history — risings, revolutions, turnings, falls. The Pleiades, the Cushmans, Raymond too — the triangular flag stars in Muriel's lap now a tiny piece of that celestial mosaic, a corner plot of sky laid claim to by his clan — who receive him there now, the last of the family, the boy at 80 now the youngest of the dead. Feb. 2, the sky arranged in triangle, a horoscope. Who can say that Delbert's course had not favored him?

Which was also, as you know, Joyce's birthday. Joyce and Delbert — two giants who possessed their own peculiar geniuses for dealing with complexity. A fathom's looped-up tangle in the twine was short work in those resolute, huge hands. Delbert's gift for the Gordian knot: consign, relegate. Heave it overboard ("They-ah!") — snarl to snail, potwarp to pearl and periwinkle at the bottom of Lobster Gut. I remember opening up the big doors to the fish house with him and clearing out that great clot of collected gear into the high water prior to moving the building. Then going back with Joan on low tides the days following to disentangle it all from the rockweed on Bernard's ledge.

Even so, Delbert knew how to dispose. I may never learn his trick — or learning the trick, will lack the resolve. Solution by deletion, by surprise — epiphanies — those tiny, fleeting conver-

gences, resolutions, that Joyce was so fond of; whose own looping lines and tangle settle out not in the Gut but in gut intestinal — complex, jewel-like, underwater refractions, words bending light in a sea of words. Reading Joyce here is like scallop-dipping from the dory in a ripple of wind. Now you see it now you don't. People were always saying: "You can't ever say about Delbert." How, for instance, he might suddenly show up somewhere — or might never (suddenly). Josephine said once: "He just stopped coming, I don't know why. A streak. Delbert's funny that way." I wonder if it wasn't just disentangling twine, Delbert clearing his deck a little. He had awfully big feet and might be needing walking space. Now I visit now I vanish. The unexpected loss for us is Delbert suddenly gone, but looming. Epiphany by deletion. Among us now by suddenly not being.

Joyce enjoyed the ground hog affiliation with his beginnings and had the date of his book's coming out delayed to coincide. I want to imagine that Delbert would approve too, with his endings — going under in good company, his own cool holing-up re-entry into the earth. Joyce as Dedalus, whose urge is to fly or to "Bloom" — to burgeon from the earth — but who nonetheless loses himself below to endless labyrinthine wanderings among the damp caves of "dear dirty Dublin." And like Dedalus in the cave, Delbertalus watched his grid of sky — through the storm glass lattice of his open kitchen door — and watched his calendar; and it was he who taught me to notice how, in January, the day's increase begins first on the sunset end and only later on the rising. "Oh, we'eoyl get some good days yet," he would say on the bad ones we seemed to save for paying him a visit.

Ground Hog Day. Joyce and Delbert divide it between them. Two patron saints — born and buried, tracking the ground hog, who travels up and back the same day. Between them the legend becomes allegorical, between birth and return the entire track telescoped, foreshortened — dreamlike — into one brief, quirky moment we know not to take seriously . . . Sudden stirring, wakefulness, to a date on the calendar — festive — a romp of some sort. Am I late? Love calls us to the things of this world. . . .

Playing dead to the world, the ground hog sleeps. Opting not for release to the sun but for return to the revel down under

— to sensuality, darkness, and sleep. To death and death's brothers; where, through six more interminable weeks of winter, he dreams purgatorial reruns, other versions of the legend. . . .

The legends of George and Theo are here, and of Ross, Harold, Gerald, Arthur — Delbert's kin. And even if Delbert shied from the coarser versions of the legend — possessing a moral, contemplative kind of detachment ("Platonic" by comparison) — I do see him as a derivative of it, of an ingenuous sort, an uncorrupted sort. Earth-bound, bound by the bay waters — gathering gulls' eggs as a boy from the ledges of the stark outer islands — there was a primal, inarticulate kind of connectedness to his life — direct, deliberate, immovable — fastened down to cleats and ring bolts. Some said a crazy streak. Delbert's mind moved when and to where Delbert coaxed it to — period. I loved, while sitting with him, the silences; then to hear the sudden thoughts from out of nowhere. The Red Sox and the Bluejays — bad pitching after he'd fallen asleep. A snake in the cellar. Bald tires — and I picture him maybe picturing himself in those enormous gentle bulls of Clydesdale horses he so admired, had driven up country to see. Friendly, goodhearted, both open and secretive — a leather-skinned, white-haired shy giant: Delbert in winter sitting in his kitchen. The oil stove hot at his back (kettle of Jacob's cattle beans — he'd said, spooned up to show — and a junk of salt pork stewing), the tall lamp's naked bulb a raw, burning spot of light that cast enormous darting wall-shadows, incongruously, of Delbert's form. . . . He sits at the kitchen table playing solitaire, not rudely, as we sit watching — almost expectantly — as though having come in for an appointment with the Tarot. "Oh, we'eoyl get some good days yet," he says without looking up from his unfolding deck — says as if in reply to some unexpressed complaint in the room. He scoops up the played-out cards with inconsequence, without hint of good or bad throw — simply as fact stated, fact done, collected, gone — like a sound heard by Cage and no one else. He needs an animal, a dog, I am thinking, a cat on the chair ignoring him. He is lifting, offering now a donut from the box — praises them; and, on his feet now, he scuffs hugely across clacky linoleum through the door frame into the dim light of the other room . . . Surrounded now by a sense of hearing the low flame's burn in the stove; and by the sense, closer — left alone in the oddly silent kitchen while he'd gone out, abruptly, for something — of seeing, knowing Delbert by his wall shadows gone.

He'd had his walls blown-in insulated and had decided against spending the winter with Geneva, and had grown lonely towards the end. Something had happened to his car and Bernard came up with a hulking dark green old station wagon with good paint (and unrecommended it to him) from his "Useful" lot. Which got Delbert out driving again and seeing his old regulars — Eaton at his traps in his harbor shack below the Factory, and Geneva and Bernard in the cement and glass house with the sod roof, and of course to the row of mostly empty chairs in the Thomaston laundromat — the only laundromat he'd ever liked. He liked a fish market in the neighborhood, too. I picture him driving home keeping his cusk and Wisk out of the same bag, minding his olfactories. The car got poor mileage and Bernard told him he'd ought to cut it in half (a piece out of the middle and weld bow and stern back together). A shame that he never did, I think. Besides improving his mileage, he could have sold the midships in New York at the *National Review* to be welded into Bill Buckley's elongated limo. Buckley would have written him into a column celebrating grass-roots voluntarism in the service of shrinking the federal deficit. Anyhow, Delbert had the right idea — solution by deletion — suitable to the nature of environs, even if the foreshortening might have set his knee bones abeam of his ears behind the wheel. Buckley's chauffeur in a good Friendship fog would not be able to keep track of back and front fenders at the same time. On city avenues, though, a long car is a help, where the traffic lights run in coordinated tiers — all red, all green. I don't pay much attention to the city, it's been so long, and we were tempted for one reckless minute to come down to Sam's opening and to see you all again, and then realized, when we started thinking particulars, just how hopelessly remote the likelihood actually was. Then Jim Freeland called up to ask about getting a new roof put on his house and reissued his standing invitation to use his place in the palms at New Smyrna Beach. It's pitiful how unenterprising we seem to have grown. Maybe it's the iron in the deep ledges here, the insidious pull-down of magnetic fields that aviators complain about in the compass when they cross the southern shore of the island. We have begun to understand how it was mainly logistics or the mechanics of making a trip that Ivan had in mind. He showed us the engraved invitation he and Jose had got in one Friday's mail to attend the opening of a show of Wescotts, Allison and Paul, in West Chester, Pa. "We'd have no more way of getting to Pennsylvania," Ivan said, "than the moon." I was deeply sorry. Of course they could. Was it the money, the car? The hens, the shop, Tinny and the aged cats? or more — for they all had simple solutions. I had been instantly charmed to imagine them standing in that gallery, looking like a Congregational deacon and his wife, dressed like a million dollars, among millionaires, seeing paintings and drawings identifiable as their home, their own world, a million miles away. But it was clear that the invitation was getting read in much the same way as he might a little item run across in "The Time" on his couch. That was not very long ago and we, alas, seem not much different now. Except for lacking in the charm they would have carried there — and we have no hens. We'd have gone off to Holly Solomon like Delbert upcountry to view the Clydesdales. It has not always been this way. I used to hop down here in the VW between classes in Windsor, pretty regular in streaks, and then drive right in to Monday morning class with the lesson all jangling around in my skull, like some sort of outlander day student up since three with a five-hour commute — Abe Lincoln trudging overland to school with his Bible under his arm. It was a religious exercise, a pilgrimage, a dream chased for the pot of gold — the uncautious yellow. But the red and green boulevard of traffic lights one learns to wake to in a fishing town are not stop / go but port / starboard, where darkness occurs less at night than in the morning, and the engines heard beyond the distant dark cries of dogs are the diesel grind of boats heading out. For all of the sea traffic followed and the boats boarded here daily, habitually — like city folks to the subway — there seems an uneasy, certain slippage in our propeller, a cau-

Jim Freeland was one of my three college roommates. He is an attorney in Orlando, Florida, and spends summers in his house on Davis Point. His son, Jed, and my son, Jesse, are good friends.

tiousness about horizons and tricks of illusion, and an instinct to be home before dark. We're getting to resemble the wary ground hog. The pull is more down now than out. Delbert is way ahead of us.

I don't believe his boat left the mooring even once all last summer. Late in December, just before the deep cold swept down, it was hauled out to Carl's dooryard for a pilot house to be built onto it over the winter and we learned then that Delbert had sold it to Norman. For a fisherman of 80 whose hands were failing him, chronically now, Delbert's deletion would seem to have been a final statement of sorts. Or at least a heavy punctuation on the page, bold ink, a period moved back by shortening the sentence. He was a lobsterman with fewer words left in his head, I think, than traps left on the bottom of the bay, and now he had sold *boat* from his vocabulary. In the ancient East, if he had lived a little longer, he'd have soon got it cleaned down to a vocabulary of one, an empty house, a donut on the table — a vowel looped up with a consonant, one single sound — and, chanting, would have levitated to heaven on his bowl of salt pork and beans. I remember Updike's conclusion about Joyce at the time of Joyce's death — that he'd seemed to have got down through his great piles clear to the bottom; that he had written what he'd had to write. "His desk was clear." Delbert had his own desk, or desks, and the final clarity would apply as truly. The two giants may have differed in style and in collectibles, but I cannot think that Delbert at the end was not equally well scrubbed of the weighty wares. What a ramble, what a jumble. Talking about one virtue and in doing it doing the opposite. . . .

Curious compensation from the cat this morning. I picked a dime out of her litter box. Tin wafer among the turds. Tipping the chambermaid — figures she gets a better position in a pay toilet. Or else it was unintentional and just jiggled out of her pocket when her pants were down. She's been reading Nobby Brown in the outhouse about how money is feces, filthy lucre — the "excremental vision" — a normal cat's-eye view anyhow and picked up Kendall Morse on the subject, I'd have found some five-dollar bills besides. I do like ducks, but Bill Hall's barnyard of a wharf is just as slick as any street I've walked in New York. Worse, I think. I carry spare keys now so that if I fumble the originals they can just stay put right where they land. Very soon now the green eggs will begin appearing again underfoot — that used to make us such wonderful, light pumpkin cakes. Bill himself even used to lead us to hidden nests when he'd find one — eight or ten eggs, sometimes more, under the mulching in his rose beds. Half a dozen in a coil of potwarp inside a lobster trap on the town wharf. More under the washboard of Arnold's boat. It was like Easter morning every day, the fishermen all keeping track and advising us. Every egg that didn't go into a cake in April made one in the end. This winter Bill's barnyard more than doubled — overnight. Word spreads outside the flock about the easy pickins over here. Bill grumbles about it surprisingly little — only perfunctorily. With his cane now and halting gait — and the white hair and leanness and ruddy face and spectacles — he has become the very image of a mission Franciscan, a father to the flock, the homeless and the needy. The ducks know the appointed hour and they flock to the shed every day well ahead of time and quack and gurgle and abide one another the waiting — until at last the door opens and Bill appears, leaning on his cane and bearing in the other hand his bucket of grains; and the ducks agitate audibly and gravitate to his feet, amass in huddles — a motley pool of feathers he is moving through now, towering above them like some graven image of an afternoon shrine come to life, in Italy, in Portugal, a mission kept for centuries on the site of an ancient miracle, saying, "Duckee, duckee, duckee, duckee . . ." in the Portugese, down from the legendary Latin. The family of attending pigeons is up to ten or a dozen now, an odd touch of the city here, a sign of the megalopolis advancing up the seaboard — and a handful of city sparrows that hang around the wharf girders — and of course the scooting cats. Bill and Evelyn are not themselves unmindful of this identity to their lives. Profits from the fuel they sell the fishermen at all hours of the light and dark suffice barely to put food on the kitchen table, let alone the bird grains cast onto the beach. Bill has said to me, "When you get too old to do much of anything, you might as well try and be of service to somebody." How would any of us get along without them right there, even as gate keepers, lighthouse people? The code beeping in on his radio in the gas shack still elicits in me a sense of urgency, or a suddenly widening immediacy, to the tiny place — the bank of equipment, the wall charts, the green digital lights ticking, the Cola and candy sold as at an outpost, the broad window that looks out east across the bay. Sense of walking onto the bridge of a ship, or of ascending to a hidden communications post in the hills of wartime. Bill at his microphone talking to Bolivia, to Tel Aviv, and you picture a map of the world, an astronaut's view of the globe with wire-thin beams of lines converging at Friendship. "All through with the gas?" Bill says, interrupting — then says to Bolivia: "My friends are here who collect the duck eggs." Ham radio people carry on the damndest chatterings. Have you ever listened to one? Backyard fence gossip whispered to the far ends of the earth — for free. Ma Bell, go to hell. Communications technology has got to be the greatest of all of our marvels. "Says he's got a peacock for a pet," Bill says to me while I pay for the gas. "It's nine o'clock there and they're having a drought. His daughter goes to the University of Chicago." The other morning when I was in, Bill had picked up an Israeli who was trying without success to raise his brother in Bridgewater, Maine. Bill copied down the brother's name and went in the house and phoned the man up to say his brother wanted to talk with him. Turn on your radio. Then he came back down to the wharf and turned it on the brotherly exchange he'd linked up. Might as well be of service to somebody. Would that our diplomats could do as well.

As for the duck eggs, we have surrendered them back to their mothers. A duck could be somebody's mother. The edge wore off our enthusiasm for light cakes two seasons ago when we got to thinking about ducks being, like others of us, what they eat. It's Bill's henyard grits, true, but it's also the harbor sewage, the storm-sewer runoff, the parking puddles. The range of these birds is extremely local — about as broad as dump rats' — having neither the control of a domestic barnyard nor the purer run of forage enjoyed by their wild cousins. If a harbor clam is a risk and forbidden by the law, then I suspect in these green eggs we were eating more of the harbor and the homes of Friendship than we cared to realize. In enlightenment, green takes on a paler tone. Even groan. Good, though.

It's all been downhill from there. Food is the new idolatry. And yes, I am afraid we are, as you say, "thoroughly macrobiotic" now — despite the awful word — macrobiotic — sounding fed-out by a computer devoted to translating Lao-tze inscrutables into the Star Wars marketplace. Yes, anyhow — we are, but afraid that if we say so you won't come see us any more, or you'll make it like a hospital call or prison visit. Or — worse — that you will come and ruin us with Temptation from the Garden of Earthly Delights. Big Apples. That's how it all began, all this wretchedness. The fall — from the tree. One bite of that unsteamed apple (too yin!) — and by Eve, a woman (yin) — a windfall of sin. Yin sin. Indulgence. Whereas the wily serpent (yang — or even whang) might in his wily wisdom have offered brown rice or barleycorn, or even buckwheat buns — something a little closer to the center of the scales; and God might not have got quite so crazy about up-setting the handiwork, the balance. The Scheme. God raging, bellowing. Too yang! Type A. Elevated BP. Throwing his children out all but naked into the desert to roam and to toil. And why? Because they "did not obey." A fit of manly fury if ever there was. Is it any wonder all this domestic violence coming out of the closet? Yahweh: Yahngweh. Yangway, the wrong way. A meat eater, too. Even after eschewing at the last minute the flesh of the tender boy Isaac — "whom you love" — and whom he'd ordered up for a roast on the high altar, what did he substitute as an alter-native? A ram! Mutton. From darkness to darkness on the chilly mountain, showing his true mettle. Mutton — calling out raspishly "Here am I" like the woozy murmur of Seduction itself. Males building a fire for meat on a mountain. Male, fire, meat, mountain: all yang. Ram is male. The substitution is consistent. He missed his chance here — right then and there — to alter the whole course. What has the 4,000-yr. history of Israel been — and thence of "the Nations," the world — if not relentless vengeance and blood slaughter (meat), outrage upon outrage, like one carnal sin committed to drive away another? The craving exacerbated, a sign of eating too yang, the hollow pit in the belly that nags after a feed. We commit violence as solution to violence. The village de-stroyed in order to save it. The war to end all war. Death Row at Sing Sing. Five bucks from the pocket issued down the shithouse in order to go down for loose change. Yahweh missed his chance on Mount Moriah. Instead of slipping the ram in in place of the boy, his greater wisdom might have slipped in a plate of sushi. Or, once in a while, for a snack, a little umeboshi paste on a rice cake, a pinch of gomachio. Our mythology betrays us; and history, like poetry, proves mythology. The way to the heart of history is through the stomach.

And so we're all about 90 lbs. or less and would blow away in a blizzard if we didn't tie our tethers down. All but Sarah, that is, whose lucky exile and institutional cookery have spared her this plague of worms. All organs interconnected, cooperating for survival as never before. Nowadays when I suck in my stom-ach every morning, lying on my back in bed, I can use my naval to check the front alignment of spinal vertebrae. Food absorption is so efficient that I find myself having less and less conventional use for the anus. It all comes out through the mouth now — as in these chronicles. With so much green verbiage excreting orally, I've been considering jumping onto the crest of this Gary Hart wave, with some truly "New Ideas" for degenerative old assholes but I am not prepared to say yet what those might be and think it wise to wait for the Convention this summer in San Francisco. The liberated energy in that good neighborhood ought to be able to nail at least one plank of new positions into the platform. The annual Halloween parade could be rescheduled to coincide and at-tract network coverage, bringing an original, lampooning side-show to the Carnival with some truly fresh ideas. Dressed up, styl-ized, prancing around reciting dogma and the lyric of self-realiza-tion like circus clowns staging Greek high drama, they would ap-peal directly to the educated electronic electorate of the baby boom culture, the first generation to grow up on TV and college — or TV in college, where soap opera is a six-credit seminar and heart-ache catalogued with a Kierkegaardian rigor. Hart and my atrophic anus know the wasted potential of the turned-off tube.

I love it. I feel like a bird getting tail feathers. When I run now, the act itself is exhilarating — like a dolphin, a deer, a kid in a summer field prancing, cavorting — is the feeling of it. I actually just plod along — but steady. It's a real little boost to me at this point — 43 and unwritten, unbuilt, and half the family leaving house and home. I think I could run all the way to Ohio. (And would get there before I could figure out why I might have wanted to.) I am not becoming a jogger, a nut. "No why, just a dip." The exhilaration will pass. Life will grind down again. No difference between before and after — only that the feet are a little bit off the ground. . . .

The only reason to run to Ohio might be to claim our baggage. Like you, we celebrated an unusual Christmas weekend ourselves this winter — though a significant step removed from the immediacy of yours. Joan's mother suffers heart spasms, and one full-blown heart attack put her in the hospital for Christmas. So we flew up to Rochester — Friday the 23rd, when the whole world was flying someplace for Christmas, and bumping, and getting bumped and bribed by Delta and reticketed on the same plane for remote destinations, closed airports, baggage gone "to Dayton we think" in a snowstorm. Logan Airport had shut down the day before and we dropped right into that great Yule log jam. Then we sat on the floor in the steamy-glassed transit room in Syracuse, with about ten thousand other Christmas migrants, watching daylight fade behind the gray snowfall while we waited for a replacement door to fly in from Newark. Our pilot couldn't work the one we had — trouble with the hydraulics. Down but no up. All out to the runway — looking now like Christmas presents in the snowfall. The atmosphere was holiday. People lined up ten deep at the pay phones to call ahead. The noise was elevating. The airplane was not, and just sat — for hours — as though staring at the crowd of us through the glass wall like a tin animal at a floodlit creche, the Adoration, a riderless horse in from the Holy Crusades — the name EMPIRE painted across its glistening, armored back. Giddy high school kids hunkered on the floor, as around a soda fountain or a summer campfire, and drank cheap champagne from the bottle — getting glaze-eyed, sexual, silly with boredom, where we ourselves decided to sit, nearby, also on the floor and — lacking only bamboo mats — to open macrobiotic supper.

The works. In plastic. Joan had brought everything. It has been our hand-luggage carried on board — pre-cooked and stacked in the order of picking down through. Plastic cups, plastic bowls with lids, plastic forks, plastic bags. The plastic thermos jug had the first course: steaming miso soup. Then rice, rice with barley, millet, azuki beans, kale, watercress, tamari-roasted sunflower seeds, pumpkin seeds, pumpkin chunks (steamed), squash, carrots, kombu, hijiki, mochi, broccoli, cabbage, gomachio, garbanzos, umeboshi paste, brussels sprouts, daikon, rice cakes, millet balls, rice balls and I don't know what all else, hairballs — and sushi by the satchelful. And a fleeting hankering on my part for a honk of the cheap champagne. Just enough to confess to, when next I should happen to meet the dark priest. And a good dram of the bansha tea. Probably I've left something out. Well, even with the best of ambience these meals generally take about two hours to eat, properly chewed, and so you might as well be waiting for a door from Newark. We were grateful for the broken airplane. Gratitude and contentment aid the digestion. Nature knows no anger. Anger: complaining liver. The unplanned is foreseen by simple acceptance of the present. And by long chewing. Chewing is meditative. We kept Syracuse entertained for an evening and likely even advanced a corner of the World Plan to a bleak outpost of darkness. You never see so many dripping pizzas and cans of Welch's Grape Juice walk past as when you're sitting on the floor sucking on another sushi. . . .

Suppers with the family were farcical — nervous, grim — hilarious. Kind of like Federico doing dinner scenes with Ingmar in the editing room.

There were puns and one or two abrupt, low-volume sexual indelicacies — jokes — coarse and undinnerly. But the wine was sloshing around in my own paunch, too, pretty well, and they had come as a relief. Not discouraged by the alcohol nor by the relief of being home again after the long, white hospital hours, Grandad had got fixated on a beef politics around the table with his serving fork. Joan's plate had an imbalance of vegetables on it and she was nursing a picked-at, unconvincing, no-thank-you portion of a chicken wing. The crumb crust of the wing was pulled into a tiny tidy pile on the plate rim. I of course had abandoned the home religion the minute we had landed there and was managing to lick up the various sweet unmentionables rejected by the rest — and which I had known, days in advance of our flight, would themselves be making the whole trip worth the effort. My apostasy was confusing to Grandad. Contemptuous of our moths and mohair diet from the start, he found me doubly contemptible for fleeing my convictions and eating exactly as he was. He had even ambushed me right off by asking — point blank, with the beef and gravy and yams all steaming in a pool on my plate — would I "ask the blessing." It crossed my mind through the fuddlement of alcohol that perhaps he had really meant his, or maybe both — his approval and God's — just as I had had to years and years before, in jacket and tie in the evening dark of the living room, over the issue of his daughter. I keep half-expecting him one day to withdraw the permit. I can remember starting out with an ambiguous "Our Father . . ." but the rest has faded now into a wine-bleached blank. . . .

So I came home and got sick for two or three days to purge the sins of my apostasy. Michio Kushi calls it (you guessed it) "discharge" — what "confession" is to the Catholic church. The cat's water bowl on the kitchen floor had a crust of ice over it and you can bet she was glad to see us. If she'd slept on it nighttimes like Bill's ducks on their eggs, that would not have happened, but cats can't think of everything. The cabbages in the cellar had suffered a little, too. They had limped up and were drying out pretty severely, and so Joan decided to make sauerkraut. And so we have had cabbage pickling in a big crock in the stable cool of the bathroom. It doesn't smell bad at all, in fact may help — in any case is surely less pungent than the cabbage house air and what all that Karen Levey had to put up with that summer in Syracuse. A bathroom seems a fitting place for a crock and you can't be too sleepy about the choice of porcelains when you get up in the night. We keep a flashlight by the bed.

And are keeping one all charged up in reserve for you, too, when you come for your new harvest of trees. Feb. was like April and March is carrying on like January. Come back quick and make it be summertime again.

_____

December 7, 1984

Can we come and see you? We fly Christmas Eve to Roch-ester from Portland, connecting Delta to US Air at LaGuardia and not Boston. Same on return trip, Thursday morning the 27th, and we can stay over in NY for no cost. Love to see you and also *Fanny and Alexander*, Bergman's movie. Otherwise devoid of specific desire, we've no idea what to do fallen into that great sweet cider-mash of a big apple. The city, even as idea, is an overload on our circuits. We have stayed away too long. Will you be there?

The bottom has dropped out of Dec., right on schedule, and in the garden we got caught with our plants down, but that's good. Beachweed mulch on the seedy thatch. We have snow, been three days thrashing in the bilges, battered around every which way in a gale of wind — E, NE, SE, W, now NW to SW to W to dying tonight, says Joe, and cold rising to the moon, the first "single digits" night of the winter. "Single digits": suggesting isolation's spread, like ice forming over still water, this hardening, fixing resolve of winter, a dwindling towards zero — the icy, fondling digits of the hand of God. It is expected to lose its grip soon, though. The weatherman this morning said: ". . . warming to the upper twenties and lower Thursdays by Tuesday." The brain tends to thicken with the metabolism. Fingers numb in insulated orange rubber gloves (I think they paint them orange to reassure the wearer of color when the digits turn white and can no longer be counted up by sensation) and in the dory, heaving with the chop swells, the chest seems oddly to lighten under the pull of cold air and down-feathers, puffed, like the breasts of winter gulls that stand on the bar and stare into the wind. A tide coming, a sea spilling high onto the beach in harder storms, this sense of everything about to rolly wholly topsy T'orsdy bass-over-sea-nettle and every year I hear Ivan saying he's not ready and that the Chinese are coming. Single digits — the loss of fingers to frostbite, like Ahab's loss of leg to a whale. "It's like having a nightmare, then you'll wake up in the morning and it's over with." Ivan was a man of faith. The blessed assurance of winter: the sun bottoms out and turns upward, and the infant summer light is born. In bathing clothes, a swaddling suit, and dazzling on your beach sand. Your abandoned summer beach, where you all so love to swim. You have left your legacy, and Siobhan her Chinese shoes for the invaders, like crabs caught high in the tide rocks. Devine Light is there now, the low, dazzling winter sunlight striking in off the bay. A woman in the news yesterday ran a stop sign whose existence she had "lost in the sun." But it won't be long now. A good night's sleep with Ivan. Summer's light is just behind the eastern sky. . . .

Ivernia had Mobil set a new storage tank in the ground underneath the gas pumps in front of the store. The Maxcys live next door and last week had to move out, find a new winter home. Gasoline has leached into their well. The fumes inside the house were so heavy that they had to shut off the heat for danger of an explosion. Now the Gilchrists — neighbors to the north — have it, as do several other wells down the street, and no one can say where it will stop. Crews are coming soon to test wells all over town and make drillings. We're an item in the papers and on the radio. The state has an extensive list of leakers. We're numbered. When you uncork your pipe next June you may find something new to tint your tea. Black gold. An oil well in every back yard, and the sun's pool of power on everybody's roof. It's an American dream — like Ivernia's winning the Plymouth on Hobson's home run. Be careful what you wish for; you just may get it.

Ivernia Wallace ran one of Friendship's two markets until about two years ago. Jim alludes to an incident on a Sunday afternoon years ago. I was on the island pulling out another stump and listening to the ballgame on a transistor radio. Back then the Red Sox had a contest called Homerun Inning. You sent in a card, and if your card was selected you were paired with a batter in that inning. If he hit one downtown, you won a car. I heard, "Butch Hobson batting for Ivernia Wallace of Friendship, Maine." I stopped. The stillness was like Casey at the bat, but unlike Casey, Hobson homered! I stood there stunned, shouting at birch trees, and trying to envision the modest pandemonium in town, where, I imagined, sunburned arms were hoisting Ivernia triumphantly above the soda cooler. To this day her license plate reads: "Sox 4," Hobson's uniform number. The following year, her mate, Archie Wallace, had his card picked, but his batter — it might have been Yaz — flied out. The next batter homered over the left field screen.

Moxie's new owners are Bob Yambor and Becky Parsons. There is activity already. Contracted major wharf repairs, remodeling the bldgs for inn, restaurant — looking to get a permit (incl. for alcohol) from the town — which might take some fancy footwork in this dry desert, this moral oasis within the soaking seascape of summertime shoshiety. Says they have 2 or 300,000 dollars' insurance just on the house. "Don't put a fryolator in the kitchen!" warned the insurance agent. Fryolators elevate the premium, big. Lucky to have heard that. We had been considering a fryolator for the fishhouse, since we all like fryolated fish quite a lot. They plan to have ready six or eight rooms by the summer — sort of bed and breakfast for a start — something like $1200 / wk, I think — or maybe it was $120 / night, I can't remember — anyhow it's some figur' well beyond where I can count to and it involves the digits 0, 1, and 2. It's this sort of perceptual gap that makes the gossip bramble so much fun to get into. They plan half a dozen little sailboats on moorings, nature trails marked around the island (staff and a crew at last, it sounds — a commission for the Road Commissioner), arrangements with Edgar for parking and regular ferry runs. Grimes doing land labor — he came out in November and mowed and then plowed up a nice big plot by the double barns for a garden — seems to be leaving his tractor there for the winter. And of course power and, they hope, regular telephones. Bob says CMP (power) will lay their cable along the old right-of-way (you've seen it on the charts — the water between Davis Pt. and Bob Pratt's) and bring power to the island if they have commitments from two customers. Bernie Lewis — who owns the pound — naturally jumped right in. Land cables will run along the ground, or under, and (I still can't quite grasp) the rest of us can tap in all around the island just as regular CMP customers anywhere. Sign up and they'll run the cable over, plug you in. Jockeying with the phone company is still incomplete but Bob thinks they'll probably end up running their lines right along with the power. Backhoes to go to work on trenches in the spring. We'll be plugged in for summer light. Electric blankets for your tents this year! To hell with the sun, to hell with windmills and gasoline and gas, the costly chugchug to drive your drill and toaster, gone the rodent-corpse odor of gas leak under Bettie's kitchen . . . My astonishment is that of a Kansas wheat farmer in 1930. My own Grandfather Bliss is said to have installed the first gas lighting in the town of Mansfield, Massachusetts — maps for the library. (Books are in my blood, you see. Or the edges of them, at least — all lined up moldering on the shelf and well-lighted.) A little initiative goes a long way out here. Energy has come back to Friendship Long Island in more forms than one. We are a throwback to the glory of the quarry days, and of the saw mill and the school house and the summer people steamboating in from Boston in their white finery. Your all-white lawn parties for a fancy price now. Better get your house built and lived in. Manos says we have a gold mine out here. About as joyfully as Ivernia's oil reserves. Property values will skyrocket. He says he will probably start renting. . . .

Well, I am not being brief. *The Electric Moxie Acid Test.* What will they name it? The Parsonage Yambor? The Parson's Rest? The Moxie Tavern? A series of framed lithographs above the hearth in the Lilac Lounge showing Major General Henry Knox's February crossing of Meduncook Strait for goose dinner and a draught of the oaken-barreled Moxie, 1794. Available for purchase in the Morse Cloak Room are copies of Ivan's book, autographed posthumously by the author by donation of the clipped bottom corners of his cancelled checks with the Waldoboro Savings.

Josephine has booked to lead the Betsy Ross parade down the blueberry field on the 4th of July, Johnny Thompson to address from the horizon with the cannon report. There's no telling how we can all capitalize on this and get the Republicans re-elected in '86. . . .

Barbara and her son Will were here late Nov. for a look at Lettie's (PL. 26) and a meeting with Atty. Davison. We'll describe when we see you, but it looks as though G will agree to sell the whole of it — and Barbara would afterwards deal with M herself over clearing the title. Melodrama of the matadors. The positioning of the bull (flops). I think of hyperbole, or of its cousin, so to speak, in mathematics — the hyperbola; its asymptote, or Zeno's Paradox. Nearer and nearer and nearer but never to arrive, to connect — to possess. Anyhow, asymptotically, it helps to plot the curve, or curve the plot and heightens interest in the infinite approach. All foreplay. . . .

Fishhouse (PL. 61) work began on Halloween and has been — how shall I say? Brutal joy. One long raw purification ritual — fall into winter — if house = body — high over that ledge, where stone, air, water and fire meet. Fishhouse: I am Jonah, then, escaping to Spain. It's not spirits that get up and charge around on Halloween, it's the body — putting other creatures' clothes on and playing at unlikely, illicit forms of being. I played at, for example, crow up there — among those crow families that hang out there in the high spruces above the beach. The view is extraordinary — the most elevating fix (to the stomach) being straight down, and most of the time there is not much to hang onto. I know now why tree creatures have curved toenails. One day last week, alone in the high scaffolding and wearing everything I could find — including two wool hats, blue downy puff of a jacket under the nail apron, and fewer sox than I would have liked (the bulk begins to have a reverse effect on the circulation) — I drifted, probably, in time into a light fog-stratum stage of hypothermia. A boundary is crossed without knowing where, precisely, or when; euphoric punishment of winter. Toes, fingers — when you can't say for sure without looking whether you're holding a nail or have dropped it. Cold, persistent grey wind off the ocean . . . feeling like a window-washer in New York watching ice form in his bucket. Slosh rhythm of rockweed in the tide below the staging plank, far below, a backdrop out of focus — grown mesmerizing now — like a nest of gold jellyfish — more felt now

---

Barbara Beebe bought "Lettie's" on Long Island and moved there from Connecticut with her daughter, Susan. They are both artists. Babara's sculptural jewelry is shown at the Frick Gallery in Belfast, and Susan's whimsical illustrations and paper dolls of animal characters and children are distributed by B. Shackman in New York. Together Barbara and Susan have created versions of Cinderella *(PL. 28) and* The Nutcracker *using dolls and elaborate sets. On the island they lead a nineteenth century life, cooking on a woodstove, lighting with candles, hauling water, and keeping chickens and bees. They have spent two winters on the island.*

than looked at — the subtle lurch and spring of the plank itself to body weight, working, hammering, bending for a shingle — a crow's weight landed on a bough. What became clear was just how simple the step over would be. That the physicality of it, of being there — the engineering of it, so to speak — reduced to one simple choice: you either step here, or step here, you will die. Then at some point crept into my mind the image of my mother and my father — dead now — risen to a perch surely loftier than my plank of lurching lumber — their arms extended to receive me. No warning of danger, no parental alarms; just welcome-where-have-you-been? My mind would push them away — shingling, shaving edges, fitting, fumbling for nails — but they moved in and out, haunting, harping, demonic in that brutal solitude, the cold. I knew, too, where the image had come from. Many years after her death, I had read it out of a sort of diary my mother had kept. Delirious with fever and near death with a kidney infection when she was a small girl, she saw her dead grandmother, she said, reaching out to embrace her, hug her — receive her among the dead. It had not been scary. But it rose to anger me on my plank up there. Belleau Gamble, when Mother used to call him in from games in the evening darkening air, and the boy calling back: Not yet! I'm not ready. . . .

The mind does not just have "thoughts." The mind has the physicality of flesh choices of its own volition and without approval — direct, simple, and without reflective fanfare. I think disease is like this. . . .

Other days are like springtime and you peel down to the wool shirt. In December the sun seems to make all the difference. The building is in the lee of the north wind, and on the right kind of day the two sides of the island — George's cove and Flat Rock Beach — can be seasons apart. Twice recently, landing in the morning at George's in whitecaps at our back, I have doubted I could even hold a hammer straight. Then got over there and within twenty minutes stood in shirtsleeves between the sun and the black paper on the wall, looking out into the sun glare towards Otter Island (PL. 14) at the wind gusts and white-feathers chop. Which is why, partly, this writing delay — unexpected good days, a surprise. We are on our own now, since Thanksgiving, but we work as steadily as when we had the crew. They were great. Staples, McNally and Merrifield — names naming their nature and the job, Merrifield coming in out of the daisies for three days on the roof. Two of us worked either side, and Joan dipped all the shingles. Herb Staples was the boss — Bettie's man. Or, we all put our heads together on the issues and it couldn't have gone better. Still, what with the high horizontal windows, the dormer to the SE, the sliding doors and rain skirt and the gable-vent hoods — I am afraid I have destroyed the integrity of the building that was so lovely. But worth it — unavoidable to some extent, I feel, in order to have happen on the inside what I wanted. Goal for you: design your house so that it comes out as right on the outside as on the inside. It's a rare building, I feel, that does both, from what I've seen. And "solar" houses are the worst — perfectly awful. Sunshine may be free for the taking, but its capture demands a high price, it would seem. . . .

Florence has retired from Sylvania. Bought a new dress for her party, and the day after New Years she and Moe took off for Florida till April. They gave us a big bright jar of jam made from wild strawberries Moe had picked last summer in Canada. You must know that we got our little barn moved over — Moe and I — from Little Island — the day after you left, I think, and we had the little picnic here with Barbara and Moe and Florence and you all. Good luck with the wind and tides, and we set it high on the

Moe Berube grew up in Canada, where he worked as a lumberjack. He ran his own auto repair shop in Jay, Maine, for years. Moe has worked for almost everyone on the island at one time or another. When something breaks or needs doing, we go to Moe. The first time I met Moe he was out on an evening walk. The back end of Jim's old truck had completely collapsed and was sinking like an aged water buffalo with splayed hind legs into the mud of a little stream. Jim and I were at a loss. Moe grabbed Jim's come-along, quickly girdled the truck with the cable, hitched it to the back end and started cranking. It was like watching a movie run backwards, the truck magically reassembling itself. Jim drove the truck that way for the rest of the summer. Moe now lives with Florence Cushman in her camp on the island April through October, when they leave for Florida.

beach below George's, then built a sort of trestle and next day with two comealongs and rollers from your woods cranked it up and over the bank and front lawn just as pretty as you please. If George used oxen for his place he'd have done it that way. You learn how the pyramids were built by getting a crew of slaves and building yourself another. Then we went by truck and rails and rollers across the lawn and brook to permanent perch west of the garden. The roof needed major restructuring — done now. And ready for the shingles.

I check into the hospital in Portland for 2 days today for an angiogram of my brain. (This winter head-work has got to stop — overload on the tender circuits.) I seized up last Tuesday — busted a kitchen chair — with a "grand mal" convulsion — full blown, cookbook — complete with the mashed tongue, rolled eyes, saliva and blood and definitive load in my pants. Joan said I yelled Whoa! Whoa! Whoa! . . . like Ken Cady on the bench. No warning to speak of. I recall studying a magazine page — words sharp, focused, clear as crystal, but it read like Russian, Polish, whatever — made no sense. I thought it was a joke issue of some sort. It never occurred to me that the error might be in my perception. Strange sensation — so objective, clear — so sure. Then recall nothing till waking in bed, staring up at Joan, Steve — having no idea of place, time, or who they were.

Sounds like Martin Luther's revelation — who met the Devil shitting in the Wittenberg Castle — bolt out of the blue — an incident with the force of a conversion. I was released from Pen Bay Hospital (Rockport) next day. EEG and CT-Scan both showing trouble. Referred to neurosurgeon in Portland. Angiogram X-rays tomorrow should pin down the diagnosis. Shadow on the left side (temple) of the CT Scan: Surgeon Brinkman says either a stroke, a contusion (bump) or a tumor. If tumor, then "low grade early stage" — whether benign or malignant — still doesn't allow much room for expansion. Will do nothing in which case. X-ray me again in 3 months. Brinkman is a Yale medical school man —

figure he must know Selzer — about the same age — bright, witty says the left temple shadow is verbal recognition. Finnegan's Wake — It was like Finnegan's Wake: word recognition but it made no sense. Do I see my future in a sequel? Dr. Williams says: Don't write your obituary yet. Dinnegan's Wake — perfect. Macrobiotics says convulsion is discharge of Yin. Fine. How to explain the picture? Settling of toxin? Discharge: Clot? Stroke? Occurred Tuesday at 2 P.M. Previous Sunday we took Sarah back to Smith — pigged out on all-you-can-eat. Fitzwilly's brunch in town — the works, everything — split and carried firewood for 2 hrs. while gorging on Harlan's shrimp — 3-4 pounds, all myself sweet as maple syrup (50 cents / lb. this year — fat, eggs, incredible, best season in years) — and sipping whiskey, a lot over 2 hrs.' work time — then white wine. Thought I was in heaven — wood-splitting in breezy, shrimpy, brutal cold of snow and moonlight. Hung over in the morning but not too long and seemed worth it. Great effortless pile of wood around the stove — matched only by the heap of crustacea in the belly. Then 2 P.M. the convulsion. Discharge of Yin would seem right. But what's the shade in the photo? It's hard not to imagine some relevance of the indulgence. (I also broke a tooth and filling that night on the shrimp — lower molar — mercury on the brain?) Anyhow, been looking for motivation to quit the alcohol and this seems it. Parched for a week. I feel great. A little heady — but am on 300 mg / day Dilantin, depressant, and this may be why? We shall see.

I have with me now 14 views of my brain — in one-centimeter slices. Walnut in a shell — see through any way you want to. For delivery to Portland Hospital lab. My inner portrait. Thought you should be here to make prints before the original be relinquished, or run to jelly. Then I thought about your negatives losing their image and figure my own organ would be in good company. Schedule me in, will you? Stephen says there's nothing much to worry about. The shadow on the negative is just another note caught up in there.

I am living in some dream, some thing here, of my own making. Discharge, release, let it go — We'll share the garble with you when this oracle decides to speak.

Johnny Neubig called last night to report the island's completed cuttings — yrs and Bettie's, and to get her phone no., issuing tacit invitation thereby to the burgeoning of summer and of course the broader lawn party. Swarthy sweethearts beneath the Sycamore in bleached cotton saris. Says the ground is frozen solid over there and no danger of a fire. I assume he means he burnt. Seventy-foot trunks oughtn't to be cut up for cordwood; the island ought to have a sawmill, he says, like in the olden days. Instead we have the treadmill, says I, and suppress out-of-season glimpses ahead at the binnacle's black balance quivering back around, a familiar breeze freshening already towards another summer's sideways slippage. The freshening of my — so to speak — navigational trades. I made the mistake of visiting the island the other day. Found everything woefully unmolested. Fingers in orange gloves all ghastly white, knuckle down to nail.

_____

1985

Augusta says no reciprocity (*a reference to a New York City parking ticket*); we may have parked with impunity. Fortunate they didn't tow us down to Tammany Hall. Country people never learn what signs are for.

WHARFUNSAFEKEEPOFF. Did you ever see anyone ever hesitate? But we arrived in the village from NY to find NO FIRES sign by the firehouse. Chief considers us dry. May keep your trees up. But unpredicted snow all day today, and maybe if J can do it soon, OK.

_____

March 1985

1:30 on the morning of my birthday. Slept about three hours. License has expired and brain's licentiousness, convulsion's remote aftermath, with a whimper. Stops in Hartford and in Portland. I am exhausted. Joan drives us in skidding up the driveway slope in hard snow, stalling, snuffing out the engine — a return to a moon-bright bog of deep winter, retreat from shirtsleeves in your city to near-zero, this windless cold of full moon — a night desert, moonscape — outrageous return to a dead-of-night dream. Bergman past midnight the night before. Death and fulmination and psychic returns, withdrawals, his railings against rage and pain and damnation and death-rattle — death by water, death by fire — God speaking out of darkness to the solitary, through a windshield-glass darkly, mad ful-moonations of a winter light. Fulminations, convulsions, suppuration, purulence, — healing by suppurating drain, the springtime purge to purification. Bergman goes to an island in the springtime, holes up before a blank wall (a movie screen without a projectionist: the church sexton says to the apostate parson in *Winter Light*: Give me a sign.) and writes his screenplay; where his devils, he says, "come out and speak to me." Hieronymus in the fourth century found them in his hideous retreat to the Syrian desert, where alone, he says, "in the heat of the sun with no other companions than scorpions and wild beasts," he watched Roman maidens dancing before him and beat his breast with a stone. His spiritual grandchild Bosch will find them turned up in the Garden of Delights, where in the left-brain side of the triptych he details a fine, illumined landscape of my skull and tumor. The innkeeper whose inn is his own body in a boat. Eggshell's bust and skullcrack. And again in the Tree-Man drawing. My mind itches for gardens, the purulent, interior sore of early spring. The final image of *The Virgin Spring*, whose psyche festers into the miracle of water breaking out from the earth where he stands. Desert and darkness, water and light. The issue in *The Virgin Spring* is getting candles to the Easter chapel in time for the miracle of light, of fire. Water bursts from the bower where the candle-bearing virgin is raped and bludgeoned. Or if not Bergman, Bunuel — whose Simon of the Desert has to have been Symeon the Stylite; who in the fifth century lived at the top of a stone pillar, a sort of candle himself wrought large, a pillar of fire by fulmination, by psychic immolation, sixty feet up over the Syrian desert, after Moses's "pillar of fire" that led the Hebrews out of bondage in the fleshpots into the desert wilderness of the Sinai. Symeon the Candle; Little Chandler. He got there, modern students surmise, on grant money, chasing stylos — housing trends for *Mother Earth News Catalog*. His true motive was nearness to god and escape from the village dogs. God-dog: Joyce's heaven-earth dyslexia. Little Chandler's mundane isolation and elevated ego-dreams in Joyce's story, *A Little Cloud* — whose epiphany is a rush of tears — a "little cloud" — over not God's but the world's "real presence." Dog-god. Stephen Dedalus lives in the Martello stylos. Joyce the Stylist; Stephen's "high priest" of art, whose God inhabits stylus, his pen — and stones the city dogs. View from the pillar of exaltation, the epiphany: "a little cloud on the horizon, the size of man's hand . . . ." The earthbound sun worshippers put to rout and slaughter, Yahweh's presence is revealed to Elijah to end the drought. I picture a night on the pillar spent restless in a thunderstorm, the hermit laid out flat on his back, on ithyphallos bed of stone slab, stark, wild-eyed, under the exacting hand of God . . . .

Mitch holding his hand above my face. His eyes are closed, as though he were listening for something; listening to something — distant music, Joyce might say. A love ditty from his youth, being sung in another room. His hand adjusting to elevations, as if by sensation to his skin, to his fingers, the hand of a man come in from the wood lot — gloves off, to warm his fingers over the cookstove. My own body lying easy, lying lazy, devoid of thought or focus, a weightless, summer-hammock's rest in shade, staring easy, upward through his hand into ceiling — overcast of the plane of plaster, a gray-white sky of a pleasant summer evening. Mitch the baseball player. He stays standing in the box between pitches, the umpire's time out to check the ball, and Mitch closing

Mitch Peritz is a close friend and a fine chiropractor practicing in New York. Mitch met the Dinsmores when he began treating Stephen for his asthma. When Jim was first diagnosed with a tumor, he was told it was inoperable and to "come back in a year." So Jim went to Mitch for alternative help, and to Michio Kushi in Boston, for macrobiotic counseling. A year and a half later an MRI showed no change in the tumor. His physicians decided that it was an infarction. Jim relaxed his diet and therapy. Several months later his seizures returned.

his eyes to gain a focus, releasing a hand from his grip at the bat — he adjusts, listens — without glancing towards the dugout; lowers his hand. An inch, maybe. It hangs in the air, in stylized, weightless suspension, the hand of a puppeteer, a curtained box in New York, off Broadway — matinees at the Peritz. The hand lowers; hesitates — probing in air; lowers still more, as if probing at layers, altitudes, intonations, densities — warm streaks in water (Is he listening: feeling? Seeing phosphenes in the sleep-dark; phosphorescence waked by the mind moving over water?). It is a priest's hand over the pool of a font. Less ritualized, solitary; a blind man finding the curb with a cane; Jesse in the bathtub tugging a sailboat on a string: the bow dips, takes on water; Mitch's hand lowers . . . to fetch; to retrieve; eliciting . . . until, eyes closing — my own curtain parts to the epiphany in a Bergman movie; and I grow aware, vaguely, of sensation in my skull, faintly — weak — as of battery current to a bell-wire across the left temple. A tic; a kind of skin twitch over bone — tic of a cat's spine — fur in a summer breeze. It is neither pleasant nor painful; and my eyes are closed now, as if for the better feel of it, or inner vision; a focus my left eye has lost as in a moment's dozing off at the theater; and I have grown aware now of my breathing. Mouth shut, eyes shut — I am pulling suddenly at air now — deeply, unexpectedly — as though involuntarily, like a swimmer's chest drawing in a river that has suddenly pulled him under. Jesse's sailboat in the tub suddenly now a schooner taking water. The breathing grows heavier — long, deep pull at air. Corinne: *Pull from the diaphragm. All strength is from the hara.* (Mitch is saying, exhale through your mouth, inhale through your nose. I don't know where his hand is; I hear Joan brush past, leaving the room.) Bell-wire sensation at my left temple, thumb at a doorbell — persistent, insistent; a spider's walk of sensation across a bell-wire dewy web — between ear and eye, but in; down under. *Come in, come in — Get the door, will you . . . ?* Joan going out. I don't know where Mitch's hand is; knowing it only by the feel now — a contact, a proximity. I do not open my eyes. I do not know whether the hand is touching my temple. I know the hand is near my face, and only that my body is pulling deep at air, pulling and letting go; again . . . like a kid wanting to get dizzy on the summer grass

— neither involuntarily nor without volition. It tastes in my nostrils, a taste high in my head — taste on bone — that I have never tasted before — pungent taste-smell of a kind of yellow-gas sensation breathed raw, high behind the eyes; but it does not burn; like pollen's taste from Frost's-nature's first green-is-gold transience of April; spruce trees in capsulated burst. Release in air, a sea-breeze drawing onto the island. Breath is cool, but deep, driven; and it is of body, chest — abdominal — but the locus is above; is my head; the locus is in the coming-in and the going-out — tastes at the rims of nostrils — teeth-edges — and lips, the yellow-gas, cool pollen sensation behind the eyes. *Come in, come in* . . . until suddenly there is a breaking open of something; a pressure from down under burst; artesian; swollen ground, water's burst through gravel. Tears welling and burst from my whole face, an eruption, eyelids squeezing shut the floodgates; bell wire spider-web of prickly fulmination in my skull — fire and water; *come in, come in* . . . until it's as if it is not Mitch's hand touching now, laid above my eyes, my foreskull, but Bergman's father of the bludgeoned virgin, the last scene, the final image of the movie, standing in the violated, broken gravel of spring, puncture of birthing bag in the barn, Jesus suddenly by surprise in the stable — my broken shell, or skull — high water on the eve of my birthday — Mitch's fallen hand to my head, where water is breaking up through from down under, tears welling up, the purulent spring rain, winter breaking into water — skull's brain-drain — flooding down my cheeks on both sides, like a sudden cloudburst drenching Gulliver lashed by little people helplessly to the beach. Tears devoid of sorrow or remorse or terror; just tears; water. Purgatorial as the breeze in Bernard's bulrushes, or farting in the fishhouse. A little thundercloud on Gulliver's head, cloud the size of Mitch's hand, epiphany's water — burst exacted — drawn out, driven out: *ex acutus* — that would put an end to the drought. . . .

He let me lie for a while, and it gave me a chance to remember staring at Joan or the kitchen floor after my seizure. A jumble . . . .

It did not happen like that. I don't know why I have told it this way; in these terms; by these images. I had not an image, not a thought in my head. I was unaware of picture or idea, aware only, as in meditation, that something was happening to me — and that I was the one doing it — but as if volitionlessly. That Mitch was there too, in midwifery.

Well, I don't know what I'm after. The trouble with Jesus's walking on water is that every boob with a ballpoint and brownie feels he's got to get it in all the morning papers from half a dozen angles. . . .

My attraction to Bergman must be that he made one movie in his lifetime from a hundred angles — the last third of them with the cryptic grays colored in, like a kid with new crayons gone back to his picture-Bibles in the old-country parsonage. Or Bach at the organ every Sunday with a new Feast Day freshening last week's chorale. Gilbert and Sullivan at the same endless dinner party, with proprieties. If I were to blather on about ecstasy in eating but never had had but one meal in my life, I don't think I could expect ever to get it just right in a whole trunkful of diaries. Which may be what Boynton had in mind that time when he told me he doubted anybody could live and write, too. Figure he must be doing a lot of writing nowadays if that's the case; and I'm getting pretty hungry myself on this diet. If Mitch is going to draw blood out of a stone again next week, he can just as well warm his fingers over a pizza in the oven while we're waiting.

The descriptions here are dripping back to drought. Fortunately. It is no longer my birthday and I did not stay up all night. Since then, Ronnie loosed his dogs on the island for rabbits and fox, and they ended up chasing down a coyote, and they destroyed it. The astonishment was general: the dogs', the coyote's, Ronnie's — and even maybe the rabbits' — vulnerable, easy, unpreferred. I've had to chase down this thing from Mitch's briar patch, it seems, and I may have destroyed it. Astonishment and a shot weren't enough of the white whale for Ahab, either. We'll all be back.

April 7, 1985

Spring snow's fortunate fall: Johnny did yr trees the very day we were in NY! You'll love the light, the openness. It's sky back to the small balsams now. Outhouse tree I never got to mark so it still stands. He took dead ones by the brook and also, unhappily, the bowed birch you befriended. Hard to get a Maine woodsman, of any stripe, to love and leave a log who's turned its toes up. I have found excellent skiff and motor for Barbara — like Ross's but lighter motor — and think she has bought over the phone, Stets & Pinkham; and also have Charley Bagley making mooring and offhaul for her. She comes May 6. Frank O. thinks she needs a power tractor for groceries etc. but machinery is trouble, I think, and feel a Garden Way cart best to begin with. Susan is tough and a mountain woman. Could they borrow yrs for a bit, to try? She won't get a mower, hates the noise, she says, and Susan will scythe. I heard from Ken Spohr at the Lilac Shop that Dan W. is ailing with the diabetes again, and alone. Housekeeper has fluid above the brain and mental flights again and gone to a home. Dan out of the hosp. now but turning folks away in his dooryard. Feeling sick, eating poorly and trouble with his vision, a diabetic thing. But Ken says, "I go down and kick him in the ass and he's got new glasses now and driving in his car again. Go see him." If I had a license of my own. Need a good swift kick, is all. North Pole to the noggin to line up the stop signs, like all those traffic lights on Sixth Avenue. Anyway Joan took me for a drive yesterday with her flu and bought 4 mint-condition pump jacks, used, from Uncle Henry's — in Searsport, two miles down a cowpasture dirt road in the rain, with more potholes than the whole jungle road network rainy season posited by the French in Gabon. The French leave theirs as a measure of political control, keeping the villagers afoot, or else flat of pneumatics without a gas station. Searsport set theirs, I believe, as a sort of watchdog for Dexter Littlefield's trailer in the alderswamp. They heard us coming — a mile off — by the rattle in Joan's teeth. The Beans of Egypt. We saved $60 on the pumpjacks and ten minutes later were back to driving past the Gatsby villas of Belfast and the dim-lit gaze of millionaires. We found red-haired Freddy working late Saturday evening on a pulled engine at Pottle's and got replaced our fugitive Rabbit hubcap from a wreck, for $3. Then stopped by in Camden to discover Fellini playing this wk at Bayview St: *And the Ship Sails On*. Will go see.

MAY 25, 1985

Barbara and Susan rooting in already. Discoveries of nice trash. Pristine floors beneath the linoleum. They have named the several rooms (PL. 27). The rose room, the lilac room, the apple room . . . according to prospect, proximity. Barbara has studio picked out — that corner room to the south downstairs with 3 windows — where you once spoke about photographing blue wallpaper. Attic is bare! Forty bags trash from it. They love your cart. We, too — Joan is getting one for b'day. B and S having Charlie Bagley rototil a garden plot, west of the kitchen. Susan dreams of draft horses someday. A barn again, hay. Rossie to come back fiddling Sat'dy nights. Moxie has a henhouse, early crowing rooster. The times do cycle like the tides. Great carriage wheel of fortune turning on these roads again. Ivan might be pleased. . . .

The moose hunt ended in a capacity kill. I drove out to Lloyd's Friday in East Friendship for 4 lbs. of fish and found the head and horns of 750 lbs. of moose hanging like overspill out of the back door his fish truck. The horns and head alone must weigh 150. Eye dry as etched glass, tongue dropped like a dog's — hounded; grey as death. The hunters are being urged this year to avoid eating the moose liver and kidneys, there are said to be found high deposits of cadmium. Curious for the foragers of the wild and virgin country. Heavy metals in the hinterland — Hannibal's Crossing, the Greenville unorganized townships, the Quebec border. The source is as yet unknown, though "acid rain" is getting mentioned. Surely then this "acid rain" is euphemism and is not solved by an extra bag of limestone to the garden.

A lovely fall here otherwise. The frost held off assault on our flowers and squashes till mid-October and we have had a long drought and mild days to remember. Unprecedented carrots. Michael and Tim came every afternoon, before dusk, the day's work being done, like rabbits to Mr. McGregor's and seized their daily three. I see them as "conservationists" — the way deer hunters are — thinning out the herd. Left to its own designs, this year's crop would hurtle to its own demise. We have not crocks enough to haul them off in, nor eyes enough to brighten with the carotene.

It's a mystery, and thoroughly unpredictable. Brian and Sterling seem now right to have sensed them young — like black-backed gulls the day-old ducklings in June. Florence's garden, not a hundred yards away, gave her barely a bunch all summer. She thinks maybe it's the soil. So she's been wheelbarrowing uphill the seaweed that catches around her wharf. Moe has had water on the knee. Where he doesn't need it, and none on the gardens, where we do. But he is off the crutches now and they left for Florida the morning after Halloween and had no one knock at the camp for trick or treat. We discussed this good-humored unsurprise before they left and remembered how marvelous were those few years when Sarah and Stephen would shuffle over to Ross's rattly door after dark, all bedeviled-up and ungiggling so that Ross didn't know who they were — or said he didn't; who then lit up all over his face and howled like a hermit when they told — those sparkly blue eyes and white whiskers. Then he would half-fill single-handedly their big brown Sampson's bags. Candy bars from the table and apples and stuff from off the shelves and of course the popcorn he'd done sprinkled fresh with table sugar. He had prepared. Then back out into the dark of night and off down the road to Ivan and Josephine's for the same. And then back to George's for a minute to empty the big bags, these twenty pounds in two visits, and then head out — the four of us — down through the graveyard to the dory tied up at the point and set out for the mainland and the distant houses above the harbor, where we could see Halloween's extra lighted doorways, promising, purposeful, like the fleshy, hot interiors of jack-o'-lanterns. Sarah was a clam one year. We ran across her cardboard shells and brown undershirt one day not long ago in the fish house. . . .

E. B. White is dead. The old master is gone from the farm, the mouse, the spider, the swan. The elements of lifestyle, the whole barnyard, all of God's bleat and spin and artless articulation under his feeding hand. Simplify, simplify . . . Professor Strunk stripping to essentials, the ones and twos, like God instructing Noah in the gathering before the flood. White dazzles because it is the simplest light, is purest because it contains all of the colors. No one can write better, ever. . . .

Two late tidbits: Dr. Knock, the dentist, phoned to say he'd found report of a Swedish study — just published in September — correlating amalgams and brain tumors: severity of the tumor directly correspondent to the number of fillings in the teeth — in double the number of corpses in eight thousand of the population. "Autopsies" they said — not "corpses." A gentler word. I think of Bennett Meyers and his death by brain tumor last spring — his massive and chronic dental work — root canals, pain and that indomitable good cheer of his. And another study dentist read relating tumors and fillings with consumption of "seafood and or alcohol." Shrimp and whiskey here, whiskey and fish / eat everything that they put on your dish . . . . And this: a greater incidence of the brain tumor Glioma in dentists and dental workers than in the population at large (mercury is suspected). My brother had his right eye removed at age 2 for glioma. My lifelong speech block; the shadow of the X-ray. Several months before she died, my mother clipped from the newspaper an article describing a Harvard study of a potent chemical contamination of some sort in her hometown — Mansfield, Mass. — in the 1930's. Maybe it's time to do a little research. . . .

(Jim had carefully wrapped and enclosed a large butterfly in this letter).

These butterflies fill the autumn air here, en route from Canada to Mexico. This one fell in our garden, at the foot of pink cosmos. We send it to you not because New York is nearer to Mexico than we be in Friendship, but because the Big Apple is another bloom of the Cosmos. The butterfly at the end of Lord Jim symbolizes, perhaps, the flight of the soul. We envy you a version of that, where you are. It is not paradoxical. I am sure that butterflies fly into the city and alight in all kinds of places, all manner of gardens, whether earthen underfoot or stone cobble, stony island — Manhattan — to Helen Calder. Flights of the soul. Could it be this that the top-hatted *New Yorker* is examining through the glass? Skyscrapers' hermetic glass is a monocle in the eye socket — lens upon lens. I sit and look out, gazing inward on the fluttering soul. I am not used to this. This sudden December cold. Gusts NW to 50, the temperature never rose above 20, all day. We're going out tomorrow to collect the cat.

Did I leave my red toothbrush in yr bathroom? Previous

visit, in Oct., the 12th St. thief got my other. My destiny all dentistry these days, it seems; all mouth. Oracular. Eruption in the verbal lobe. The word; locus of trouble. and of love's stuttering letterings to you-

---

FEBRUARY 1, 1986

In fact I am waiting for film footage and reviews of my now-notorious head baked last Wed. into the magnetic meatloaf in Bangor; the very preliminary word (while putting my shirt on after an hour in the oven) favors infarction — left temporal lobe, just aft (not in) the verbal locus, and "no clot." Or no causal whatever-it-was; is gone. Toxins, metals — can they see those? Can a tumor cause an infarction? The good news is dead brain. Athena's footprint where she sprang in birth from Zeus's head. Perhaps I have given birth to something. I know now why magnets are made in the form of horse shoes: I have a gift-horse in my head. But am back in the saddle again from my tour of the underworld, and it feels great, the leather to the loins.

FEBRUARY 2, 1986

Monday night in the single digits here. The cat moves in with Michael for the duration, to pose nude for the illustrations. She will forget who we are and won't even look up from the stove and will prefer Florence's rodents to our own. Florence and Moe are rumored to be hating a heat wave in Fla and won't go out of the house. Bill Hall says you can't have everything. Last week's southeaster on the new moon was a wash: flotsam on the town wharf parking lot (broken steps pounding the sea wall), surf to the fish house woodpile, an altered beach line for Deep Cove (Adelbert to author another affidavit), and a new lawn of Gut beachsand for Bernard's green house. That mightiest of spruce trees, by yr clothesline, fallen towards the tents, asking for conversion to lumber and a house. Things are falling in place, it would seem.

MARCH 5, 1987

We lunched (as they would say) with Sarah last weekend at her restaurant. Her own pea soup and humus, and no ordinary fare, these.

Scrod in "Japanese bread crumbs." (Susu tells of the Boston cabbie whose out-of-town fare inquires as to whether he might know a "good place to get scrod." "Sure," says the cabbie, "but this is the first time I ever heard it in the subjunctive pluperfect."). . . .

It's the third day of snow today, and (lightly today and yesterday) there promises to be plenty for your camera. Groin-high; cooling — Leopold chilling the quiff. You've a bed here as long as you like, and whenever — whether Steve's vacation or not. Michael has left, to do spring renovations on his Oxford cottage. Susan will join him in April, and will see how she likes England life. Barbara works at her jewelry, and her mid-life translation to this island seems indeed to have been providential for her. She remains attentive to her aboriginal nativity — a native to all this — in a former life. A totality; a committing to it her own peculiar energy and focus. One can't not admire her — for the playing out of dream and fantasy. She set up her dolls and stuffed creatures for morning school, and presents them with a daily problem: "Today, class, we shall do penmanship." Then tomorrow it's European history. Ballet. Botany. Soon we imagine a lecture on AIDS, and safe-sex kits. For X-mas we gave her a copy of *Dogue* magazine — a parody of *Vogue*. She loved it — "perfect!" she cried — perhaps too much, and she has a dog now. A little parody of dogdom, named Fiona. Who has a bed in a cage-cradle by the parlor stove, and has joined the class. The class's problem became housebrokenness. Conflicts enter her life and elude her, graciously vanish, like drafts through a leaky farmhouse. In deepening solitude one learns to dress up, and keep active, and be of good cheer. Last month she set out for Connecticut to collect her puppy from the litter — the "little bitch" she called her. Seth made it a birthday present (Feb. 11th). The dog is a Welsh Corgie, Post's dog, you remember — Drift — who used to arrive in the amphibian like Caesar over the Alps, heroic and diminutive, old, aged, having sur-

vived hip surgery and with an unfocused gaze through cataracts —
and slightly out of control now, thenceforth shitting everywhere
the length of the wharf catwalk with the air of a visiting lord sensing something amiss with the estate — and looking you straight in
the eye from three feet below, with Merritt's foxy eyes, screaming
the runt's scream, a watchdog. A BelchCorgie, that belly laugh of
Post's. And so Post's ghost has returned now, reincarnated, for another go-round here, on Barbara's farm. Barbara assures us it's
not the breed but the training. . . .

You city people, lacking silence and the sense of an inter-
dependence among farms, don't know the joy of charting misery
over one's neighbors. It stirs the blood, gets you out of bed in the
morning, deflecting your mind from your own neuroses. My insidious, fading flu has grown pale and boring, and we are probably running out of firewood. Even the news is passively numbing,
overly interesting for its nausea. Joan read the other day where as
many as 20,000 deaths by lung cancer may be laid directly to radon gas in the home. This place is poisoned — earth, air, and water. Build your house out of concrete and don't eat; nurture the
spiritual life, find God. We are entering a new Dark Ages, including plagues. Farm families with burgeoning germinations, rampant
lymphomas, from generations of up-in-the-morning farmers satu-
rating the fields with nitrate fertilizers. We name our mistakes and
carry on, like Reagan, as if confession retracts them, humility
heals. Listen to your tumors. Don't drink water from the pasture
spring — or, for that matter, from the dooryard well. When lilacs
last in the dooryard bloomed. The days of wine and roses are over.

Woodhouse (*therapist*) is a persistent thorn, a whole crown
of thorns, a prick, a wood splinter of pain driven deep. He keeps
trying to break my rigidity ("You are a kind of prisoner . . .") and
I am masochistic to keep going. Tears expiate nothing, purge not,
wash only my feet, like Jesus' by the woman's hair — sweet, pre-
cious innocence — after coming in from the brutal desert. Joan
and I go together now.

But this is only part of it, only a fiction of the pain, a half-
truth. I am unreliable in this mood, wherein the writing itself takes
over and defines the tone. It's a sign, I think — this adulteration
— that I need to be doing my fiction. I am joining Barbara's

schoolhouse of stuffed animals. I feel a little like Boynton chroni-
cling the events on Stone Island — weeks after, looking back (I
have written almost no letters this winter) — himself quite alive,
picking away, knowing that "Helen" is soon to be drowned. The
fact is, there have been no tears for many weeks, perhaps months.
Woodhouse's gift of thorns is a deep blue rose, a flower I'd never
seen before, its fleeting, intoxicated scent a moment's self-awareness. I seem to need it to be cut into a "still-life," isolated — a
kind of fetish, brooded over — before wishing it to root again.

Sometimes when I consider prospects of not getting better,
I probe, absently, with my thumb — like a rosary — the pearled-
over tip of my right-hand middle finger, where the nail has recently, unaccountably, resumed its growing in. It's like running
across old written accounts of things shoved off unfinished, or letting March flies out of the fishhouse. Fingertips, to a reflexologist,
are brain-related. This is the one I smashed bloody and black in
the sliding door of our bus while pushing back a load of barrels,
three years ago this May . . . and I am cheered. Is this grace? A
sign? Am I here? Fingernails are known to grow on corpses. There
is the part of me that would nurture the nail on the bloating, tot-
tering corpse in me, the Boy of recent years, prior to the wake —
self-ravaged, angry, settled in — a kind of prisoner to conflicting
pulls. It is always mixed, and Boy knew that if anybody did.
Ginny gone to Sunday church — Boy in the trailer at the kitchen
table with the Governor's Club, smoking, presiding, more or less
drunk — just him and the Governor — and so having time for us,
you and me, who had appeared on his doorstep from out of nowhere. "She's a bastard and a son of a bitch. But she's an awful
good woman though." At the wake — touching, hugging —
Ginny was beautiful, hair, the eyes, the countenance as ever, the
same. Boy lay before us, and — though adjourned now from the
kitchen to the parlor — presiding still. His hands, pudgy and idle,
lay in a loose clasp on his belly; mortuary crow's feet around the
eyes, the slick mahogany hair — that helped let you see the boy in
Boy, of 1950 — Yvonne said, "Daddy was an awful big man, and
most of it was heart." They are a beautiful family; and they were
all there, huddled around; and I wanted in the end to see Boy, expecting swamp mud on his head and a bulldozer, look up and see

flesh in George's sunlight and all this love and say, "Hey! This ain't bad!"

March 4, Ash Wednesday. The beginning of solitude and denial, uncomprehension and atonement, the day when my father-in-law begins his annual liver-rest, for Jesus in the wilderness. It works. A miracle, after so many long years of brutality. God gave us livers and cats in order to prove the omnipresence of unconditional forgiveness in this world. One can't be so sure any more. It's terrifying to feel one's foothold slipping into the slough of doubt. The cat's claws are unmerciful, and she is jealous of her turf. We have forty days to figure out the good riddance of this winter. What could be more fitting than that your house be under way? — Russell's raising, sticks risen, buds swelling in your green studs, the sap running from your maple tree in the dooryard, when all flesh shall "see it" together. Bob Yambor drives around with a sticker on his car saying he "saw it" at the Waldo Theater. Flesh, one presumes — and in the tawdry gloom of winter. Now you see it, now you don't. Springtime seems to call us back to the woods — to the moist air, the light, the blooms au naturel. "See it," — all flesh, the budding spring — I feel, means something like "see to it," or "see that this spring thing happens." We really have missed something, I feel, not having had the whole village over for the rite of barn raising, for all flesh to "see it," this communal theater of the raising up, like an island birthing, this resurrection of the body — *Love's Body*, if Nobby is right (that one's house is one's body) — the hearth, the warm, womanly embrace of spring. Think how quickly the New Geo's would have gone up. Yours will spring into full bloom, ours grown almost by inflam-

Russell Carter is a carpenter who has worked on countless buildings including the local post office. At age 65 he agreed, probably foolishly, to build me a house on the island. There were never more than four of us working at a time. He did an amazing job in difficult conditions and was patient with my ignorance and idiosyncracies. His son, Lanny, installed the propane lines and lights. For the last few years, Russell has been the live-in caretaker at the Moxie Thompson place, which John Armstrong recently renovated, complete with solar power.

mation, a slow swelling, a gnawing, a tumor. After all this deep snow one flower, suddenly — the Deep Cove Easter orchid: the fleshy pink ladyslipper we look for on the way to the fish house.

————

1987

On the way to fishhouse now to prepare. Panic is over Johnny N's sudden plan to plaster tomorrow and Friday. Mainland mud is such that he can't get in to the regular job. What has a front has a back. I am so excited. This gift of a finished studio from out of the blue and Johnny's kindness, his own idea. Maybe now I will need to write this summer. If I am not going to cross the line, somebody else comes to nudge me over.

————————

APRIL 10, 1987

Johnny came out to the fishhouse yesterday, got a good helping of plaster on his pallet, and said that he's been on "Jim's diet" lately. When he didn't eat the plaster, I said, "Birdseed, then?" and he said he hasn't had a Mountain Dew in two weeks. Janet found some oil of evening primrose in Augusta and Johnny said it puts the heat right to his legs, that he can feel the difference. Says he's been eating a lot of vegetables and not meat. So come dinnertime we sat either side of the little potbelly stove (fired up to cure the plaster) and shared Janet's salmon pasta salad; and for dessert he had a fruit yogurt and washed it down with a little box of cranberry juice that you can stick a straw down into. I had a miso vegetable leftover soup and he declined my dahlia root tea because he doesn't drink coffee. I remember how his father Jack liked to grow dahlias so, and how he gave us our first tubers, for Geo's garden. So we sat there like a couple of war veterans pulling up each other's shirt to look at scars, proud of ourselves for vanquishing the devil dogs. . . .

He says the State has closed the entire state of Maine to clamdiggers because of pollution. Last week's floods scrubbed out too many city sewage tanks into the big rivers and brought the tide up a little on Flat Rock Beach. The season is open now for the shoreline harvesting of toilet turds and condoms. This washout is said to have been the worst flood in a hundred years. Driving to Woodhouse's on Monday, to Farmington, Joan and I saw Water Street houses in Augusta with great mounds of clothes and rugs moved out onto the soaking, silt-gray front porches, while front-end loaders were on the lawn scooping up rubble into dump trucks. The sight and stench brought my stomach up. It was like suddenly opening into the torture yard where prisoners of conscience were standing naked, staring at you. That snow pile you remember on your front ledge decided to vanish all at once, together with about two weeks of April shower. If your young seedlings like to get their feet wet, they'll like the ambience here just fine. Your raised bed was an inspiration. . . .

They just said on the radio that President Reagan finds the lapse in intelligence security at the US Embassy in Moscow to be the result of the failure of American schools to teach right and wrong. I think it's because you're on sabbatical this year letting people get away with things and I quit teaching right and wrong years ago, when those Marine guards were just urgent little schoolroom-Tom Sawyers, pinching Becky's bottom. The TV preachers teach right and wrong every day, right through your tube in your bedroom, but didn't see where Scripture told just how very much it cost King David to loose his loins over a bathing Bathsheba on a Florida hotel roof. David paid with the life of his child from the consummation. Modern church practice, of course, approves birth control, and Jim Baker's PTL lawyers had to think of an alternative mode and set aside $165,000 of viewer donations to rebuild the lady's virginity and keep the preacher guiding us in President Reagan's old-time principles.

See you soon — either hereabouts or thereabouts.

FEBRUARY 1988

Picture the photograph you sent of Joan standing wading to the shins (PL. 59); invert the greys, convert the pool, and you can imagine what Geo's cove has looked like last month — your

dark sweet-soak softness gone to white bitter blast. But that has all gone out now, of a piece, in a warm south storm (all but Joan, that is, who had foresight enough to anchor down). And we are open again to beach and bay. Still, the water and mud are so cold this late in the winter that the return of a good cold snap could close it all up again; you can't count on it. I won't forget the winter that the first solid shut-down was March 1st everything locked up as far as the eye could see — and it already getting into sap-sugaring days — and we couldn't get across to school. Aroostook County shuts down school in October so families can dig potatoes. There are more things to achieve than by blackboard, and I think Sarah and Steve kind of liked the strandedness and sweet suck of hardship.

But the thing that has really opened life up for us this winter — comes in your other photograph: all those thousands of bricks and a central fire. I don't know whether you saw us yet with the blanket gone between the rooms in December — but it suddenly became a house then, open to the eye and shared light and to free passage — no longer that old sense of living shut-down in a camp. The great mass of shower brick and Russian-style flue is really fabulous for heat distribution, both horizontal and vertical. There is a kind of softness to it, to heat by hot bricks — very pleasant, unscorching, intimate somehow the way a foot-soak is in a warm tub nighttime in a howling gale — and after we get our solar panels for a little power we'll put up a casablanca fan to improve the circulation even more. The first loft — NE, by the stairwell and broad glass — is my favorite workhole, as you can probably guess, for reading and writing — partly because eight-foot elevation makes it as cozy as summer barefoot, and so its just footskin and undershirt and broad low sunlight flooding in off the snow and not much time to dream of New Smyrna Beach. Sleeper, by the way, has promised the solar work for March 1st — the week he comes out to resume operations for John Armstrong (who Edie says has been birding — in among other places — Antarctica. He's not letting the moss grow underfoot). Russell and Frank and Boy's two boys Bubba and Timmy have been tearing into the place since New Years — 7 A.M. till dark. Briggs by the way did a first-rate job in finishing Jim's place and I suggested he get him to build his darkroom. Jim had asked me to check over his work, and I was sad to find, bound up like straightjacket on the lawn ledge, your X-mas tree. No takers. Either folks already had theirs or else they consider the search and cut and hauling into the house essential to the ritual. Nancy even confessed that Richard had decided to "do it right" this year. After moving his family to the land of a billion balsams and spruce and pines, he spent $26 to bring home the only Christmas tree he has ever bought in his life! When loveliness litters the landscape, perfection sticks its foot in the door.

Nor indeed can we find a week's home for our cat. We've tried everywhere and refuse to commit her to a kennel. So Joan has built her a little cat house. Aloft, nested, exposed to sunny-day sun — and with access. To outdoors, I mean. (I feel like I'm selling real estate.) We both think she'll be quite happy, and the isolation and mounting fear that we have finally abandoned her to terrible trials may feed into her fantasy and save her from boredom — as even now while we are around she amused herself with ants by the stove, brought in and hatched in the rotten firewood. A mouser's decadence. She can inherit the disturbance of some of my own dreams: the rototiller frozen into garden earth, hopelessly — deep, immovable — like a Studebaker in a junkyard. Barbara's bees burgeoning, swarmed, darkening the sky like dragonflies pledged to pollination; and the fishhouse filled up with fish — all things in their places, and benign — though overwhelming [these bee and fish dreams uneasily suggestive of Old Testament imagery (e.g. the manna) or N.T. patterings from the Revelations — or of Bergman's imagery as in the *Virgin Spring*, or of richness, or indulgence, splitting open, as it were, in any Fellini — not entirely comforting, to say the least — despite the obvious promise, the wealth. Interesting that you find Nobby turned to Islamic Apocalyptic themes — "Apocalypse" being Greek for "revelation." And the dream that Joan is pregnant and will give birth next winter back of George's, in our Away-in-a-Manger workshed by the outhouse. And the dream that Woodhouse finally has had me committed to the prison farm in South Warren, minimum security, making lobster license plates; and no softball team until spring.... and on and on. What seems striking is the consistency of the images. The language, the punning mistakes that dreams do, the ambivalences (e.g. lobster as supreme among delicacies, yet a terrifying, demonic, scorpion kind of creature; and on "license plate": the licentious platter; and finally even the comical commitment to all of this, the absurdity, the mock-seriousness, the kind of legislative joke this is to superimpose little buggy lobsters on our bumpers. Not to mention the issue of return to my livelihood in another form.) I have found my punishment in the plate shop.

The most recent dream: Devines are feasting with friends around a long table — probably longer than Thanksgiving; friendly, jovial — though I happen not to know anyone else. Introductions, joking, warmth, handclasps; and one says to me (a stranger): "Hey, how's it going?" I shrug, and say, "Up and down . . ." and he says: "Well — catch 'em while they're up."

You are wearing a white-creamy sweater with thin stripes at the neck: green, gold, blue and red — like a Ted Keller bowl....

What's comic is comic and I don't always do very well timing the catching — maybe waiting too long and it begins to slip, or grind. Johnny Neubig has a positive diagnosis now — more plaques on the MRI than before; M.S.. Dan Winchenbaugh with a couple more toes gone to the diabetes, and blinder; and he has committed himself to a nursing home: just gone — simply walking away from house and stuff and barns. And perhaps George wrote you that Charlotte has died — and the admonition, the wish, to "enjoy every minute of it." Catch 'em while they're up.

APRIL 16, 1988

The part of my scratch you couldn't read said: Buy yourself anything but Giacometti. But I have a history of being bailed out to enlightenment of one sort or another by you, and would love to have a look one day when next we are in the city. Joan loves Giacometti. One of the regrets in fact I had of Stephen leaving Wesleyan was his missing Paoletti's Art History. A mistake of my own I have since regretted — except for the fun of long ago here and there to galleries behind you to gape like a yokel. I love your photo of her on the obverse with "Harvey" vaccinated into the

shoulder flesh and figure her to be Stephen's N.Y. girlfriend un-
abashed about former passions. Will show Elwyn. All these things
have happened so quickly. I seem to be laying low from doctors of
all sorts until the fabrication of fantasy delights gets me on my
back in the script and a machinery, like the director finally getting
to Dublin on the Epiphany. It took Huston 80 years. And it
turned out right — was worth it — numbering himself among the
genius dead if Joyce weren't enough. Snow is general all over Ire-
land. Is this happening to you? Except for the temperature, we
are getting as much snow storm this minute as we had all winter!
Big spring flakes driven right up Geo's cove by NE gale of wind.
Florence and Moe arrived as brown as coconuts Thursday from
Fla. with a big bag of fresh oranges for us to snack on. None too
soon with them, too. The promise of sun — Yet . . . But Wednesday the universe came together in tide, wind, and sky (high moon,
calm, and clear) to chance our huge glass to here — and it
worked! Our skylights are in! The bathroom one clearing 200 lbs
up the roof. They are perfect, dropping right in place like the 3/4-
court swish-shot I once made in the freshman basketball game we
lost by 30 points. Instant heroes: Michael and I for all that anxiety
of design and carpentry. Wait'll you see them. Bed to square under
the bedroom one squaring the Big Dipper — like Otter Island
(PL. 45) posing for the fishhouse. This morning's delight is sitting
under the flake's soft settle — like the landing of white cats' paws.
The best luck about the glass is that now we (incl. Moe) can finish
the roof shingles (PL. 57). And Tues. the Brickmen return to resume — big house-chimney, barn chimney, and down to the
shithouse. It's not raining but what it blizzards. We haven't seen
more than her car yet at Edgar's but will ski up to Barbara's after
lunch. Her crocuses last week were dazzling. Snow is slushed up
on the tide half way to the offhaul.

Can summer be far behind?

JIM DINSMORE

PHOTOGRAPHS

Pl. 3   Down the Stairway / Friendship Harbor

PL. 4   JOAN, JIM, STEPHEN, AND SARAH DINSMORE IN THE GARDEN / FRIENDSHIP LONG ISLAND

Pl. 5   In "George's" Grass / Friendship Long Island

PL. 6 IVAN MORSE'S SHOP / FRIENDSHIP LONG ISLAND

PL. 7 JOSEPHINE MORSE / FRIENDSHIP LONG ISLAND

PL. 8   ROSSIE SIMMONS / FRIENDSHIP LONG ISLAND

Pl. 9   Rossie Simmons' Camp and a View up the Gut / Friendship Long Island

PL.10   HAROLD BENNER IN HIS SHOP / FRIENDSHIP

PL. 11 BEYER SHIP LEDGE

PL. 12 OUR CAMP AT DEEP COVE / FRIENDSHIP LONG ISLAND

PL. 13   JESSE ASLEEP / FRIENDSHIP LONG ISLAND

Pl. 14   Sky, Light, Otter Island

PL. 15 PEAR POSING / FRIENDSHIP LONG ISLAND

Pl. 16   Sunshower / Friendship Long Island

Pl. 17   Path, Light / Friendship Long Island

Pl. 18   Whiteley's House, Hopper's Shadow / Friendship Long Island

PL. 19 PURITAN MEAL, FREELAND'S COTTAGE / FRIENDSHIP

Pl. 20 Whiteley Apple Tree / Friendship Long Island

PL. 21   INTERIOR / FRIENDSHIP LONG ISLAND

PL. 22 CHEVY, DORY, SKIFF / FRIENDSHIP LONG ISLAND

PL. 23   JOHNNY NEUBIG'S CAMP / FRIENDSHIP LONG ISLAND

Pl. 26 "Lettie's" / Friendship Long Island

PL. 27   SUSAN BEEBE AND SIOBHAN IN SUSAN'S STUDIO / FRIENDSHIP LONG ISLAND

Pl. 28   Audience at the Beebe's Doll Performance of *Cinderella* / Friendship Long Island

PL. 29   Cod Cove Antiques, Route 1 / Wiscasset

Pl. 30   Route 1 / Waldoboro

PL. 31 ROUTE 1 / WARREN

PL. 32 ROUTE 1 / WARREN

Pl. 33   Outhouse / Friendship Long Island

PL. 34   ROUTE 1 / THOMASTON

PL. 35   FRIENDSHIP DAY / FRIENDSHIP

PL. 36 ROD PRATT'S BACKBOARD / FRIENDSHIP LONG ISLAND

Pl. 37   Jesse Swinging at Jed Freeland's "Snakeball" / Friendship Long Island

PL. 38   TWO BABES IN OUR COOKSHED / FRIENDSHIP LONG ISLAND

PL. 39   SIOBHAN / FRIENDSHIP LONG ISLAND

PL. 40 SPARKLERS, DEEP COVE / FRIENDSHIP LONG ISLAND

PL. 41   SIOBHAN, JESSE, JENNIFER AND BECKY AHLEMEYER ON FLORENCE CUSHMAN'S WHARF / FRIENDSHIP LONG ISLAND

Pl. 42   Lobster Pound / Little Morse Island

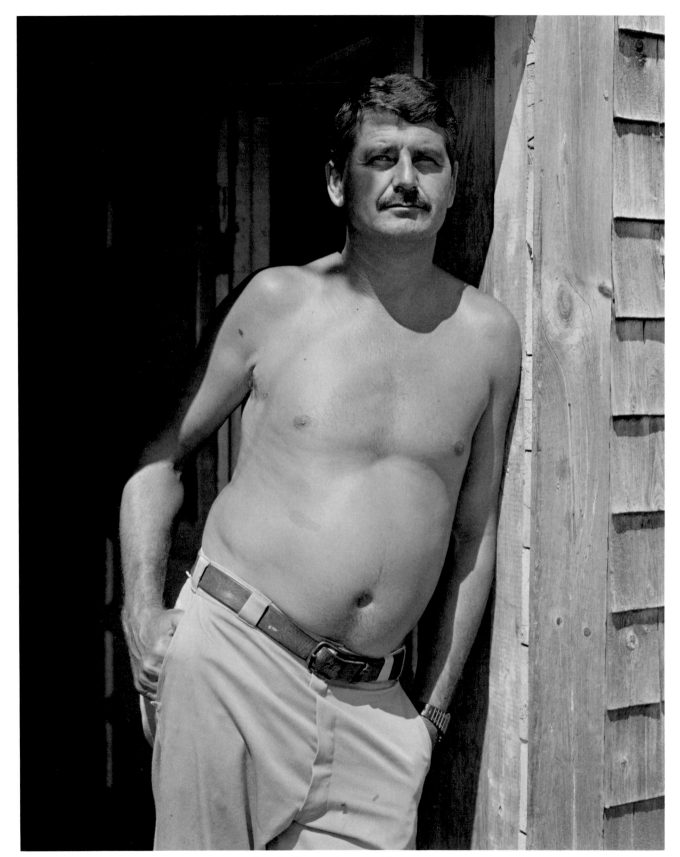

PL. 43　RONNIE SIMMONS / FRIENDSHIP

PL. 44   MACKEREL / FRIENDSHIP LONG ISLAND

Pl. 45 Otter Island

PL. 46   IN THE GUT / FRIENDSHIP LONG ISLAND

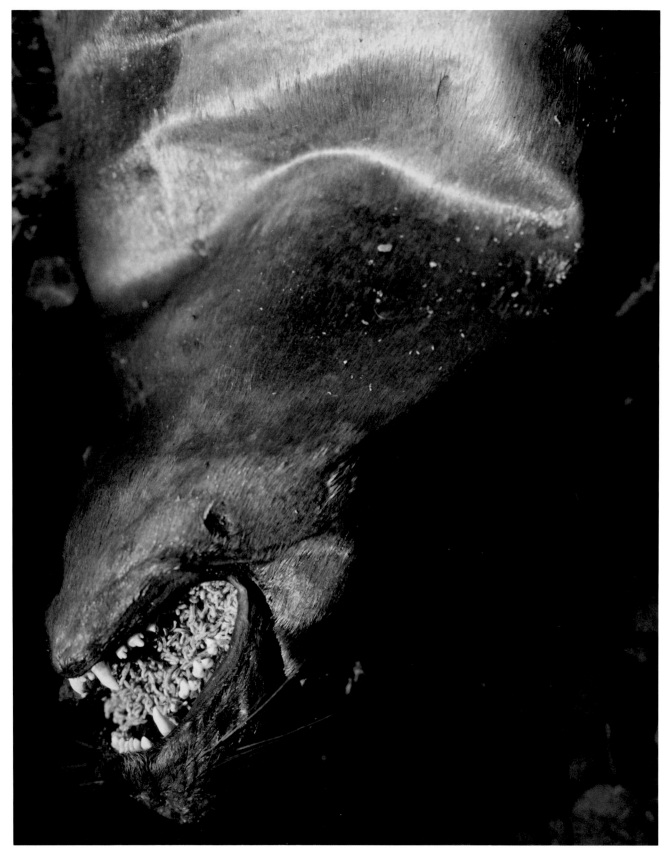

PL. 47   POOR SEALSBODY'S BODY, FLAT ROCK BEACH / FRIENDSHIP LONG ISLAND

Pl. 48 Deer Parts / Friendship

Pl. 49 WHALE VERTEBRAE / FRIENDSHIP LONG ISLAND

PL. 50   DAVID NEUBIG / FRIENDSHIP

Pl. 51   Summer Gloves, Winter / Friendship Long Island

PL. 52   NOVEMBER WOODS / FRIENDSHIP LONG ISLAND

Pl. 53   Jim's Milling Remains / Friendship Long Island

Pl. 54 Beyer Ship Ledge

Pl. 55 *Mutiny* / Friendship Long Island

PL. 56 JIM / FRIENDSHIP LONG ISLAND

Pl. 57 "George's" when Jim Died / Friendship Long Island

Pl. 58 "George's" from the Front Door / Friendship Long Island

Pl. 59 Joan in the Cove at "George's" / Friendship Long Island

PL. 60   JIM'S WRITING DESK IN THE FISHHOUSE / FRIENDSHIP LONG ISLAND

PL. 61 JIM'S FISHHOUSE / FRIENDSHIP LONG ISLAND

PL. 62   ROUTE 1 / WARREN

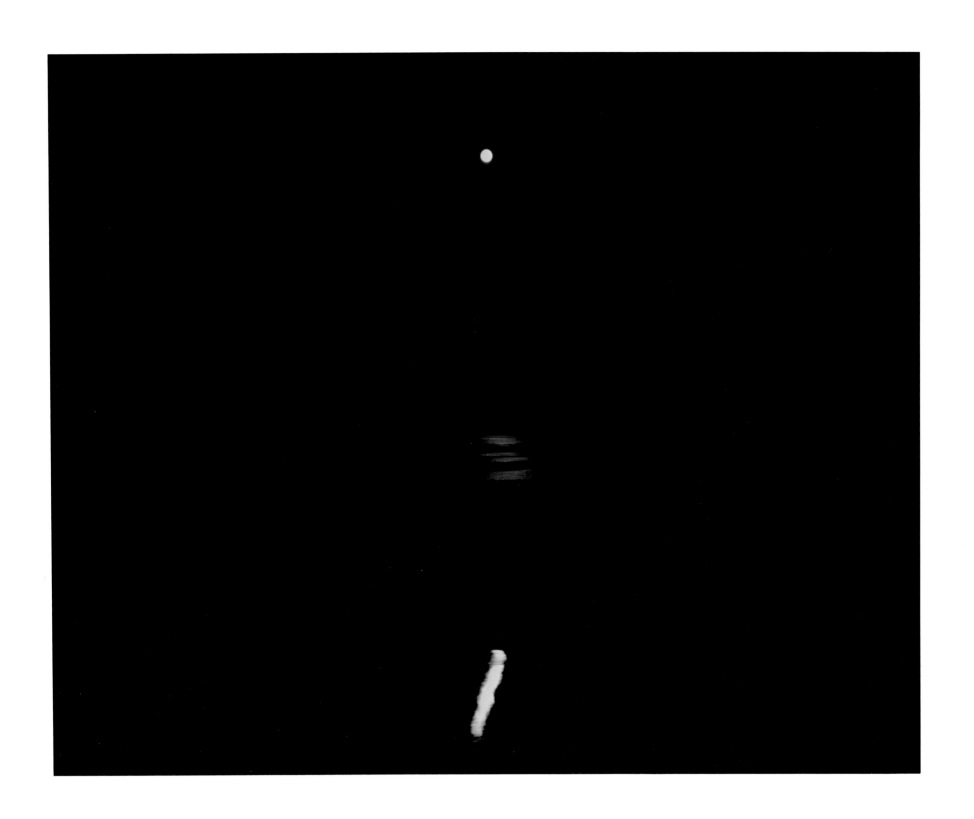

PL. 63 MOON, REFLECTIONS, DEEP COVE / FRIENDSHIP LONG ISLAND

PL. 64 UP THE STAIRWAY / FRIENDSHIP HARBOR

"Oh, we'll get some good days yet."

DELBERT CUSHMAN

ACKNOWLEDGEMENTS

I am indebted to the Guggenheim Foundation for its support of my early efforts on this project.

My friend and dealer, Bonni Benrubi, has been, as always, generous and patient throughout the making of this book. Melissa Hotchkiss, Bonni's assistant at the time, initially brought many of these photographs to Suzette McAvoy, curator at the Farnsworth Museum, Rockland, Maine, for the summer 1994 exhibit. Margie Carlo transcribed Jim's letters, some of which were hand-written on the brown wrapper covers of *New Yorker* magazines; she somehow managed to keep them in order. Paul D'Agostino spent hours cleaning up the copy on the computer-scanned disk, and made revisions everytime I changed my mind, which means all too often. Owain Hughes, Simon Pleasance, Michael Borst, and Beverly Weinstein all read unedited versions of Jim's letters and made valuable suggestions. Sam Cady, Harriet Shorr, Regina DeLuise, and John Watkins looked at various versions of the sequence of photographs and the final order and selection is due, in part, to their input. Peter Devine, Emmy Devine, Jim Freeland, Marisa Hansell, Tom Judson, and Sharon Kleinberg have generously contributed in a variety of ways. Joan, Sarah, and Stephen Dinsmore have been enthusiastic and loving in their support of this venture. I am grateful to all of you, and hope that this *Friendship* will be as good as ours.

I want to thank my parents, Ed and Liz Devine, who have from the start given me the space, time, and encouragement to make things. This book would not have been made without the help of my brother, Mike Devine, who played this game like all others — without flinching. A special note of thanks to my son Jesse, and my daughter Siobhan — my most insightful and candid critics, and my greatest blessings.

Finally, it has been my good fortune to work with designer Edith Allard, copy editor Devon Phillips, and Tilbury House's publisher, Mark Melnicove.

Cheers.

Designed by Edith Allard and Jed Devine
Duotones by Robert Hennessey, Middletown, Connecticut
Typeset in Monotype Sabon
Paper: LOE Dull, 100 lb. text
Printing by Meridian Printing, East Greenwich, Rhode Island
Binding by The Riverside Group, Rochester, New York
Production and editorial direction by Mark Melnicove
Production and editorial assistance by Devon Phillips,
James Elmendorf, Lisa Reece, Lisa Holbrook, and Amy Smallridge
Office and warehouse management by Jolene and Andrea Collins
Mr. Devine's wardrobe by Levinsky's

Tilbury House, Publishers
132 Water Street
Gardiner, Maine 04345

First Printing

Library of Congress Cataloging-in-Publication Data
Dinsmore, James J.
     Friendship / letters by Jim Dinsmore : photographs by Jed Devine.
          p.   cm.
     ISBN 0-88448-137-9
     1. Friendship Long Island (Me.)--Social life and customs.
2. Dinsmore, James J.--Correspondence. 3. Devine, Jed, 1944-   -
-Correspondence.   I. Devine, Jed, 1944-   . II. Title.
F27.K7D56 1994
974.1'53--dc20   93-37896
                                                             CIP